Praise for *Take the Leap!*

"Heather McCloskey Beck rocks a great life. She walks it, she talks it—she's the real deal. When I first set eyes on her she absolutely glowed with vibrance, exuberance, and inspiration. If you want to be that kind of person, read this book. Heather will show you how to create a life that will make you feel joyful, inspired, and deeply fulfilled, every single day."

> —COLETTE BARON-REID, bestselling author of *The Map*, CEO and Founder of The Invision Project

"Heather McCloskey Beck is a spiritual visionary. Read this book and feel your life transform in amazing ways."

> —PAT BENATAR, four-time Grammy winner and author of *Between a Heart and a Rock Place*

Take the Leap

Do What You Love
15 Minutes a Day and
Create the Life of Your Dreams

Heather McCloskey Beck

Conari Press

First published in 2013 by Conari Press, an imprint of Red Wheel/Weiser, LLC
With offices at:
665 Third Street, Suite 400
San Francisco, CA 94107
www.redwheelweiser.com

Library of Congress Cataloging-in-Publication data:

Beck, Heather McCloskey.
  Take the leap : do what you love 15 minutes a day and create the life of your dreams / Heather McCloskey Beck.
    pages cm
  ISBN 978-1-57324-589-0
  1. Self-realization—Religious aspects. 2. Inspiration—Religious aspects.
3. Vocation. I. Title.

  BL629.B43 2013
  646.7--dc23

                     2013016512

Cover design by Jim Warner
Cover photograph © Lonely/shutterstock
Interior by Maureen Forys, Happenstance Type-O-Rama

Printed in the United States of America
MAL

10 9 8 7 6 5 4 3 2 1

Standing in our own center,

recognizing our intrinsic beauty and abilities,

we are emboldened to go out into our linear lives

and express our true, Creative Essence—

without hesitation, without shame, without embarrassment.

We must acknowledge our essential right to choose to be exactly who we are,

despite any external force persuading us to believe otherwise.

Perception and belief create our human experience.

Formulate your thoughts with clarity and brilliance.

Create a life you desire to actually live.

Deepest Gratitude
to Caroline Pincus and Jan Johnson,
for their desire and willingness
to publish Take the Leap.
I am honored.

Eternal love and gratitude to my radiant
Guide and friend, Cherish

Contents

Introduction

I have always been searching: searching for an understanding of that intangible, mysteriously compelling Essence that seems to reside at the very core of my being. I have held a profound desire to comprehend that which has no physical form, yet whose intrinsic energy is the underpinning of all that I know as substance within our physical world.

Throughout my life, I have been drawn to experiences that made me feel joyful and inspired, which compelled me to discover those things that would expand my energetic self into an even more elevated state of exuberance. As a young girl, I had a profound desire to play musical instruments, sing, compose songs, and write poetry. I discovered very early on that while engaged in these creative activities, my sense of joy and wonder would increase significantly, and the more deeply I was immersed in what I was doing, the happier I became.

I also noticed that these ebullient moments were far too often fleeting and unpredictable. When I was practicing my piano, it didn't necessarily result in my feeling excited and inspired. It wasn't always fun. I was working at it, sometimes struggling, trying to improve. But what I did discover was that after practicing a piece repeatedly, there came a point where it stopped being *practice*, and quite spontaneously, I was catapulted into an experience of pure joy, as I felt the music radiating out from within me. I then discovered that by composing my own music, not only did I feel this excitement while I played the songs, but that I felt this high even more intensely when the music was my own. As I became immersed in what I was doing, I would lose my sense of awareness of my surroundings, no longer feeling separate from the piano and the music I was creating. I was streaming in a blissful state, and the piano, the music, and I were inseparable.

I was streaming in a blissful state, and the piano, the music, and I were inseparable.

So, what was this feeling, this happy, buoyant energy that seemed to be a natural part of me? I had always been the kind of person who awakened in the morning with a lovely sense of well-being, eagerly anticipating the day that lay ahead of me. I loved to be with my friends, play, compose and play music, and I loved to laugh. I never was able to get enough of things that were funny; I was always looking for more. As a child, I was at ease with how my life was unfolding and always felt quite *normal.* However, as I was busily being a *normal* kid, I was experiencing something else highly unique and very difficult to describe.

Beginning at about eight years old, as I would lie in bed at night before sleep would descend upon me, a great awareness of what I can only describe as *Presence* would seep into me, triggering within me a feeling of deep relaxation and peace. I felt entirely suspended in a gentle solitude, with my mind cleared of any thought whatsoever. I was simply there. And then, from within that peaceful place, I would begin to experience a sense of magnification and my little self would begin to expand. Cocooned within that sublime state, I grew larger and larger until I felt myself become the size of my house, then increase to the size of my waterfront town, to the reaches of Long Island, unfold to the dimensions of the United States, and then exponentially amplify to the expanse of our Earth. The more I expanded, the more content and blissful I became. While of course I was still lying in my bed, I was completely unaware of any physical sensations and instead felt myself to have no bodily limitations whatsoever. The larger I was able to become by degrees, the more joyously blissful I became in Essence, until I was simply no longer just little Heather, but rather I was part of everything that existed within our universe. I felt a wave-like infusion of love pulsating through me as I floated in a vast and elemental energy, having no sense of time or space at all. Of course, I wanted to stay there, streaming in that feeling for as long as possible, but in truth, I had no control over any of it; I was simply along for the ride.

....

The more I expanded, the more content and blissful I became.

,,,

After a while, I would feel myself returning to my *normal* self, lying in my bed. Snuggled under my covers, I continued to sense the residual presence of that enormous, wave-like energy. No longer, though, was I only Heather, the particular, individuated self, but now I was also part of something far greater in that vast wave of energy. I was aligned with the Essence of our very existence. I would always try to hold on to that remarkable feeling for as long as possible, but the familiarity of being in bed in my room, with all my things surrounding me, invariably drew me back into my customary child awareness. During the years that I enjoyed these expansion events, I noticed that if I did not interfere with this process, instead allowing this thing to unfold on its own, that I was able to remain in that state for increasingly longer periods of time, which was pure joy for me.

It wasn't until years later that I recognized just how similar that joyful feeling of streaming expansion was to the sheer pleasure I felt while playing my music and writing poetry. As I blossomed into a teen, I also recognized another variation of this feeling, when I tumbled into those first devastating moments of falling in love. Later on, I found my way into meditation, which offered me yet another means to experience this joy of streaming energy. I recognized there was a common thread among these experiences that was essential for me to understand. I felt Called to play music and to write, to actively love other people, and to meditate, hoping to be able to reconnect and be fully present with that unidentifiable Essence I had experienced when I was young. I longed for the relationships with my creative arts, with other people, and with the world in which I lived. I yearned to be able to merge with that intangibly powerful and mysteriously wonderful Essence that I had experienced when expanding as a child in bed.

....

I felt Called to play music and to write, to actively love other people, and to meditate, hoping to be able to reconnect and be fully present with that unidentifiable Essence I had experienced when I was young.

....

The message was clear: When I actively engaged in my art that inspired me, when I was romantically in love, or when I was meditating, inevitably I would lose all specific sense of self, of time, and of my surroundings, instead becoming fully immersed in the pleasure of what I was doing. I realized that I was, in fact, experiencing something very similar to what I had enjoyed as a child when I was spontaneously expanding. The truth was that I was attuned to the Essence of that which I loved and felt compelled to do, and by doing so, I was streaming in sheer exuberance, and I *loved* it.

At about the age of eighteen, I decided that I wanted to live my life feeling inspired and excited in a very conscious way. I knew that I wanted to be vitally happy, feeling that creative energy moving through me. I began to wonder if it would be possible to feel this alluring exuberance not only when playing a Steinway concert grand piano, but equally when doing my laundry, as well. I wanted to know if there was some way I could intentionally create that joyful experience of childhood expansion, on demand, regardless of where I was or what I was doing.

And so I set out to discover how to call up this exuberance within myself and weave it into my daily life in a sustainably consistent way. I launched myself into a journey of health and diet along with a variety of spiritual practices, some of which are still with me today. I studied creative writing and literature in college, which I adored. Music was my constant companion, and I practiced yoga and developed a passion and in-depth knowledge of exotic tropical plants. I had kept a journal and written poetry from a very young age and continued to document my journey through my writing, in a variety of forms. I discovered the stimulating pleasure of drinking black tea while avoiding the pitfalls of doing drugs. And not to be forgotten, there was the intoxicating rush of young love, with each relationship teaching me something new and valuable.

....

And so I set out to discover how to call up this exuberance within myself and weave it into my daily life in a sustainably consistent way.

....

By the time I was in my early twenties, I knew that I wanted to teach, write books, and eventually speak publicly about the things that mattered most to me. But I also felt that I needed to live enough of life to warrant my doing such things, so I set out to do just that. I tried to remain vibrantly awake, consciously responding to anything that offered me glimpses into that mysteriously elusive joy I had experienced as a young girl. Most often, I would awaken to my days feeling inspired by the opportunities that stretched out before me, but even while feeling positive and enthused, there were "mistakes" that awaited me, casualties of an illness that was brewing within my body and the subsequent choices I was to make.

Actually, I became a bit lost along my way, and though I still had a general idea of what I desired to do, there were times when my actions didn't reflect this understanding at all. I found myself settling into activities that held no apparent connection to what was really meaningful to me, and stranger still, I was spending time with people who really were not all that interesting. There was the allure of immediate gratification and not having to work quite so hard, and though I knew I was off-track, I found it difficult to redirect my actions. Yes, at first it was exciting to live on a Chinese Junk and sail the northeastern seaboard of the United States, but after a short period of time, I felt misdirected and empty and knew I hadn't chosen well. I was also aware that climbing onto the back seat of that Harley Davidson was a bad idea, and when I hit the pavement at 60 miles per hour and my right leg shattered, there was no doubting that I had ignored the signs. My misguided choices held an unexplainable energetic push of their own, yet simultaneously were companioned by a contradictory sense of inertia. Mysterious, indeed.

As it turned out, I was being dragged along by an undiagnosed and incapacitating illness of hypothyroidism, which created the murky framework that defined my mid-to-later-twenties. Truly, each day felt like a terrible dream that I was wading through in slow motion, yet somehow I never lost faith that I would find my way back to me. After forfeiting six years of my life to the illness and being compromised for far too many more years, I was finally diagnosed with Hashimoto's Thyroiditis. It had nearly killed me.

Remarkably though, within three months from beginning medical treatment, I began to feel well again. Step by step, I worked on rebuilding my life. I started doing things that I truly loved to do. Serendipitously, I found an opportunity to fulfill a lifelong dream: I worked on an Arabian horse ranch, riding up into the mountain creeks on long summer nights and down onto the beach in the cool morning low tides. I was thrilled and felt as though I was doing exactly what I should be doing, and my body and being were responding beautifully. I knew the difference; I had no doubt. The medication, combined with feeling joyful and happy, helped me to find my way back to health again. My passion for living was, once again, set afire.

Within a year, my husband and I had our first beautiful child, with two more glorious babes to follow, and over the years to come we raised our three amazing children in a very simple and natural seaside environment. We were a very close and loving family and my husband and I spent many years devoted to creating a home that supported our family's happiness, health, and well-being. As each child grew and expressed unique interests —*baseball, music, ballet, dragons*—I weaved my creative inclinations into their activities of choice so that we could spend time together. I often ran the music programs in my kids' classes and schools, and I wrote and recorded music for their age groups. When our kids wanted to play baseball and softball, I became the president of Malibu Little League for several years and focused on creating an emotionally healthy and positive environment where boys and girls could play ball. It was a fascinating experience to guide thirty teams of coaches and players through the playing seasons, emphasizing the philosophy of kindness and respect rather than a competition-at-all-costs ideation.

Simultaneously, I chose a career in real estate sales, in lieu of becoming a writer and musician, as it offered me the flexibility to be with our children and still provide our family with additional income. Immersed in an ultra-high-end competitive market, I developed a successful business and, most importantly to me, I maintained my philosophy of kindness, respect, and cooperation in all my transactions. Though there were many years when I could only do my writing and music sparingly, I discovered that engaging in what I loved to do for even just fifteen minutes a day made an enormous difference to my personal happiness and overall sense of well-being.

Now our children are mostly grown and I have truly lived a lot of life. There isn't a day that I don't awaken feeling inspired by the opportunities that stretch out before me, excited by how much more there is for me to do. Now, through my writing and speaking, I am able to take what I have learned and share my ideas and experiences with people from all over the world. Because of the brilliant opportunity to connect with others through social-media platforms of my choice, I now am able to reach hundreds of thousands, if not millions of people every day, from all around the globe, with my inspirational posts, interviews, online workshops, and talks. Within Facebook and Twitter, I have built communities for creatively soul-searching individuals, and now together we are engaged in a global conversation. Every day, we are discussing our collective yearnings for tapping into our creative essence and living lives we truly desire to live and how this becomes a pathway to personal and international peace. I address our creative passions and personal blocks in positive and supportive environments. I love to invite people to share their hopes and dreams, creative talents and abilities, so that they may discover the strength and inspiration within themselves to actually create a life they truly love.

Every day I receive messages from people asking me how they can change their lives and become happier, more fulfilled people. I am deeply touched to hear from those who have already begun their journey, sharing with me their joys, successes, and gratitude. But the truth is, I am truly grateful because I have found deeply rewarding and fulfilling work. I have discovered that which Calls out to me, encouraging me to help others find their way, so that they, too, can fulfill their inspired purpose for living.

Please understand, in many ways my life hasn't been easy, and yet I am thankful for every experience, both delightful and harrowing. Why would I feel gratitude for having suffered severe illness and the heartbreaking loss of loved ones? The simple truth is this: Because I have experienced extreme challenges within my life, my capacity to be a more humbled and tender human being has grown. We are often reminded that life can be complicated and messy, and our paths are not always straight and true, but we have the ability to choose kindness and compassion in our actions rather than becoming condemning, judgmental people, soured by circumstance.

How blessed are we to witness the sheer magnificence of a glorious sunrise or the sacred moments of a breathtaking sunset? Within these astounding and fluid rhythms of nature, we are reminded of the promise and possibility of the creative powers that are inherently present within our elegant world. These are simple, yet dynamic reminders, which serve to ignite the glowing embers of our own creative talents, inspiring us to get busy with creating a life that we truly desire to live. As for me, I am joyfully leaping into my next cycle of living, as I embrace what I call my "Four-H Club": Heather, Healthy, Happy, and a Hundred. I have a lot of work yet to accomplish within these next forty years, so that by the time I have become a Centurion, I will be fully reunited with that wonderful sense of Streaming I experienced as a young girl, as I touch each moment with a sense of awe, inspired by its joyful grace.

In the weaving of my life, I have been motivated by an unwavering desire to feel creatively inspired and soulfully happy. I have always wanted to know just what it was that ignited me to become awash in a symphony of sheer inspiration while I was writing poetry. From what magical portal did my intense desire to play piano emerge when only three years old? From where did these inner urgings originate? Why have they always Called out to me? I have lived in ardent pursuit of this experiential knowledge, so that I might better understand the purpose of my life and the nature of who I am. A miraculous amalgamation of passion and biology was never answer enough. Intrinsically, I have always known it was much bigger than that.

Note to Reader: As you read *Take the Leap*, I would suggest you keep a notebook or journal close at hand, so that you may write down your thoughts and responses as you make your way through the three sections of this book. Additionally, I highly welcome each of you to share your ideas and inspirations with me on my Facebook pages and/or on my website, whenever you desire.

The addresses are:

https://www.facebook.com/HeatherMcCloskeyBeckAuthor

https://www.facebook.com/TaketheLeapBook

www.HeatherMcCloskeyBeck.com

PART ONE

Leaping into Our Lives

It is from within the center of yourself that you radiate outward,
creating how you would like your life to be.
It is essential to do what you love to do.

1.

The Leap

A Tale of Possibility and Calling

We stood in a circle, infused with the exuberance of youth, foolishly blinded to the challenges we would face when we arrived, though we had been forewarned. We were briefed on the peculiar nature of the environment of where we were headed, one which was far more dense and sluggish than anything we were accustomed to.

We were told that once we left home and entered this new place, most of us would no longer remember where we had come from, nor that we had ever existed anywhere but in that new place where we would find ourselves. They said we would become unequivocally integrated into our new lives, with little hope of preserving any recall of the current moment. The challenge we had all accepted was to go there, each fortified with our own unique abilities and talents and then to call upon them, or perhaps answer to their Calling, bringing them into a form of our own creation and design, into that place where everything was possible, yet nothing was easy.

We were to choose a Guide who would watch over us, paying close attention to our physical safety and general well-being. They would assist us by facilitating introductions and connections, arranging serendipitous events and all things oft considered coincidence. They would collaborate with us so as to successfully accomplish our intended mission, offering hope and support to us in ways unseen. But our Guide would stay behind, leaving us to venture into this new, physical world unaccompanied and quite alone.

Yes, we knew what our mission was. We were being directed to craft a life that we would love: a life that would be the creative expression of our true Essence of pure consciousness, placed into a Form of density and physicality. With our uniquely creative genius, coupled with our consciousness of Essence, we were to become an integral component of humanity, each person bearing an internal directive to live a life of inspired meaning and value. By embracing our talents and abilities, we were about to live a life that Called out to us.

....

> By embracing our talents and abilities, we were about to
> live a life that Called out to us.

....

We collectively scanned one other, hoping to etch the memory of this moment and each of our dear friends' unique spirits into our consciousness, so that should we be fortunate enough to cross paths while there, we might recognize at least a flicker of that beautiful, kindred energy.

With the help of our Guides, we selected our circumstances, our families, and the architectural framework of our new lives. Reinforced by our passionate Callings that would serve as beacons of light on our new path, we heard a fluttering of gentle assurances, felt a powerful push, and then we Leaped.

2.

If Our Tale Be True

Yes, we leaped. We leaped straight into these precious little bodies, and if this tale be true, we leaped into the architectural framework of our new lives, with all the exuberance and joy that defined our unlimited and Essential Nature. We leaped with an enthusiasm born of possibility and promise, into the life we had attentively prepared for ourselves. Locked and loaded, we were inspired to get busy, to begin crafting a life that we would love, reveling in the freshness of our uniquely physical and creative abilities.

But as the story goes, physical life didn't quite match up with what we had imagined, and it appeared that we had a great deal to learn now that we were here. Though we still had one foot dipped into the collective, quantum Wave of our non-physical Essence, we had, indeed, *Particulated*, and stepped with our other foot into the individuated physicality of life in Form. We found ourselves bound by the laws of gravity, driven by a deep and profound need to connect with others. We quickly discovered that we were no longer masters of our own expansive beings, but rather, now we were babies born into the arms of our newly acquired human guardians, our parents, who were charged with tenderly caring for our disoriented little selves. While some of us were fortunate enough to be welcomed by loving mothers and fathers into safe and comfortable homes, others of us were not quite so favored, having to struggle with trauma, illness, violence, and poverty.

Yes, we had been forewarned that we might easily forget all that we had known in Essence, but who among us had truly believed it when we had stood together, poised on the brink of a fantastic and highly creative adventure? Who among us could have imagined that we would slip into this new story line of physical life so completely, so utterly unaware of what had preceded all this? We were humans now, and whether we alighted into the safety of love or landed in an exposed and dangerously vulnerable environment within this foreign world, we had arrived, and this world had become our instant reality.

Swiftly, we were swept into the ebb and flow of daily living, busy with the basics. Eating and sleeping, sleeping and eating became the most compelling activities we engaged in. Day by day, our little lives continued to unfold, as we were drawn into the perpetual routines of survival and social enculturation. Preoccupied by what was directly in front of us each and every day, we were lulled into this business of living, progressively forgetting that we had come here with an inspired plan of our very own. This bustle of life became an insidiously powerful force, silently seducing us into a repetitive rhythm of insistent activities, which was swiftly becoming the platform from within which we were navigating our lives. Day by day, we became increasingly immersed within the perspectives, values, and belief systems that were integrally woven into the fabric of our new family's cultural patterns and traditions, forgetting that we had a plan to craft a life of our design. We became so entirely involved in our new stories that we were no longer attuned to that quiet Call from deep inside of us, beckoning and whispering to us that we had come here with something very important to do—*something much bigger than this.*

Ah, but good news! Isn't there always a redeeming and omniscient kindness hidden in every good tale? We were not just left on some random doorstep, as if abandoned by a negligent parent, to single-handedly hold to our own plan—*a plan we were no longer even aware of*! Though most of us no longer remembered, we still had our Guides to support and encourage us along our new life's pathway, to remind us that we had a purpose and a beautiful reason to be here. They were here to be our constant companions, helping us to navigate the twists and turns, but more importantly, they were here to ensure that we accomplished our life's mission: to live our truest purpose. Our beloved Guides knew the beauty and brilliance of our innate genius intimately well, steadily maintaining their singular focus of helping us to recognize and embrace our gifts, even though we had become entirely blinded to their very existence. Though they would remain cloaked to our conscious awareness, it would be our Guides who would help us to navigate within this new environment we had leaped into, encouraging us to live our Calling and to craft a life that we would truly love. A tall task, indeed!

Theirs was a quiet, yet essential gift, of orchestrating seemingly serendipitous meetings and facilitating adventitious connections on our behalf, while helping to ensure our safety in a world that could be so confining and unforgiving. They were to be with us every step of the way, tenderly nudging us back toward our true pathway when we strayed too far away from our treasured, yet forgotten goals.

And what of these goals? What really had been our reason for wanting to come here in the first place? Before we Leaped, we had asked our Guides what was so desirable about leaping into one of these little human lives.

"Ahhhh," they had responded. "Life is a highly creative act! When you Leap into being human, you will experience your first creative act within the physicality of life—your birth! The reason for living is to create a life that you desire, in all its beautiful, creative physicality, a life that is a brilliant reflection of your truest Essence. The purpose of Leaping would be to live that life and create it in accordance with your own passions and desires. You would be using your talents, your unique genius, say, as an artist, to paint your joyful appreciation of beauty into your worldly canvas. If you are to become a musician, you will share your song of love, and if you will be a poet, your verse will couple heart and soul in a rhythmic dance of words. Your goal will be to express yourself in the highest and most beautiful of ways! Now tell us, do you desire to take the Leap?"

We knew our answer. We were exuberant, inspired, and ready for adventure! So, as our tale continued, with the Wave of Essence slipping away into elusive memory, we became consumed with moving into our individuated selves, connecting with our world, and yielding to the framework of our life. However, as we grew from babies into children, some of us were fortunate enough to have the opportunity to play, as all children love to do. Within our minds, hearts, and tender young bodies, our imaginations were free to wander as we dived into the joy of creating our own stories and games and developed our unique interests in those things that called out to us. Little did we realize then that through the brilliance of our imaginative play and the pursuit of our developing interests, we were aligning ourselves with our own true Essence, paving the way for our creative Calling to be ushered into our world.

Companioned by our Guides' assistance, we began to experience a taste of why we had taken the Leap. When we were left to ourselves and allowed to simply be, little masters of our own making, we experienced something deeply primal and precious. Within our private world, we were free from censorship and criticism, unencumbered by values imposed upon us by outside influences. We felt unfettered and free to express ourselves in our own uniquely creative ways. Whether it was coloring with crayons or playing music, running around wildly or cozied up reading, whatever it was that Called out for us to do, that is what unequivocally made us happiest. We instinctively knew the imaginative activities that made us feel vibrantly alive and connected to the most essential part of ourselves. We felt joyfully inspired, unlimited and free.

It was a beautiful thing when we had the opportunity to play. We became entirely unaware of our physical surroundings; the passage of time held no meaning for us at all. We were Streaming within the exuberance of Being, temporarily released from all perceptual awareness of our life's framework that we had Leaped into. Though this was merely the beginning, we were to eventually understand that these simple pleasures would serve as pre-encoded beacons for us, indicators that would call out to us and help direct us along our life's pathway.

It was from within this incredibly important opportunity to play and express our creative selves that we were able to reconnect with who we were in Essence and experience the confidence and joy of becoming a reflection of our truest nature, only now in physical form. It was from within this delicate alignment that we could almost hear the whispers from our Guides, encouraging us to continue, urging us onward to do what we loved. This was our challenge and this was our goal. It was our mission to tap into that which we loved to do and then create a way to weave it into the fabric of our lives.

....

It was our mission to tap into that which we loved to do and then create a way to weave it into the fabric of our lives.

....

However, as our Tale told us, life doesn't always allow us to weave these threads of creative joy into the tapestry of our lives.

Far too often, life has a way of sending us along detours and pathways constructed by the perceptions and patterned behaviors of those presumably responsible for our welfare. Our families, teachers, governments, and religious traditions, the structures that have been culturally and socially in place throughout all history, hold a powerful influence over our human lives, oft times interfering with our very own original plan.

Just how were we going to navigate these dips and turns along our pathway? How were we going to take the possibility and promise of living our Calling and make it become a commitment that we could fulfill? How were we going to live a life that we would truly love?

3.

Musings

Have you ever wondered what it would be like to feel happy and fulfilled, to live a life directed and guided by your own natural inclinations, your own creative interests, and personally impassioned ideas? Have you ever felt the stirrings of some deeper desire or sensed a hidden purpose residing within you, but couldn't quite figure out what that might be? Perhaps you might recall an exuberant thrill that raced through you as a child, as you were immersed in doing something that fascinated you and held your focus.

Was it a cool splash of raindrops on your face as you dashed home on your bike, or the smell of a cinnamon-apple pie that you baked with your grandma? Maybe you can recall the blissful feeling of building with your blocks or dressing your dolls, or the resonant warmth of the first musical note you played on the piano. You may have imagined yourself to be a knight in armor or a fairy princess, a great soccer player or a prima ballerina. Whether you were playing dress-up, making model cars, or immersed within a colorful spectrum of imaginary games, you were uniquely inspired, though very likely you never thought of it in this way. You were just a child, immersed in being a kid!

Life was simpler then. We didn't have to think long and hard about what we wanted to do. Quite simply, we had the ability to just give it a try! We didn't need lots of toys. All we had to do was *imagine*: imagine that we were parachuting from a plane into a lush, damp rain forest or deep-sea diving off a tropical island, in search of hidden treasure. Our imaginations ran strong. We were highly inventive and always found a way to make our stories feel vibrantly believable, as we experienced the wonder and possibility of whatever adventure we had created for ourselves that day.

Whether you were playing dress-up, making model cars, or immersed within a colorful spectrum of imaginary games, you were uniquely inspired, though very likely you never thought of it in this way.

When I was five years old, my best friend and I played endless games of galloping on horseback throughout the mountains and riverbeds of the Rocky Mountains. But of course, there were no mountains or rivers to cool our horses' wearied hooves where we lived. While the North Shore of Long Island was a beautiful place to grow up, it was flat as flat could be, with no running river in sight, no horses stabled in our backyards. All the same, it made little difference to us. We felt expansive and free, employing a miraculous mixture of imagination, impassioned spirit, and determination within our play. We were not attuned to a droning, rational voice whispering to us that our games were impossible. We were young and fresh and it hadn't occurred to us to wonder if we were capable, deserving, or good enough to play in these adventures. We didn't evaluate or assess our activities. These were not our concerns. Playing was something that came naturally to us, in the best and most pleasurable ways, and as children, we did it really well.

Have you ever thought back to a time when you were little, and remembered something that you loved to do? Try it now. Take a moment and let that idea simmer within you. Allow yourself to drift into one of those special memories. Do you recall how time seemed to stand still and how you had little awareness of the world outside of what you were doing? How did you feel then: warm, contented, inspired? Likely so, if you were relaxed and free to enjoy your play. It is actually quite remarkable to reflect upon these earlier times. Did it ever occur to you that within these profound, yet simple childhood pleasures resided a hint of what you would deeply desire to do within your life as an adult?

Did it ever occur to you that within these profound, yet simple childhood pleasures resided a hint of what you would deeply desire to do within your life as an adult?

When I was in elementary school, I knew a boy who carried a toy doctor's bag with him to school every day for six months, insisting that we call him Dr. Smith, rather than Randy. Not at all surprisingly: Later, as an adult, Randy went on to become a family doctor. Looking back on our lives with the brilliant clarity of hindsight, many of us have known people like this: the kids who just always knew what they wanted to do, from the time they were very little. The boy who was always out on the baseball field until long after dark went on to play college and pro baseball. The little girl who loved to play dress-up had become a very talented fashion designer. Think back in your life and see if you remember someone from your childhood who always seemed to know what they loved and wanted to be when they grew up, and then actually did it!

Have you noticed now, as an adult, that it is the simple things in your life that seem to trigger those special memories of your childhood that quietly reside within you? A warm brush of wind on your face might remind you of a time when you stood in awe, gazing out over the sparkling expanse of ocean. Perhaps a slanting ray of sunlight ignites a memory of how you stared up into the sky, marveling at the architectural majesty of the skyscrapers that surrounded you in a similar light. Maybe it is a sweet melody that reminds you of your first piano lesson or perhaps your first kiss. How amazing that these small events can hold such power within them, igniting such compelling emotional responses within us.

What Did I Want to Be?

Do you remember being asked what you wanted to *be* when you grew up? This was often a question my teachers directed to the class at the beginning of a new school year. It was also considered a good opener by other adults who really didn't know us all that well. What did *I* want to *be*? Well, at eight years old I wanted to be a symphony conductor, a pianist, a singer, a teacher, and I also wanted to be a baseball player! In high school, it was my desire to be a folksinger, writing my songs and poems and performing them to anyone who would listen. By the time I had entered college, I wanted to earn my doctorate in literature and teach at the university level, while writing books and speaking publicly. Couldn't we do it all?

....

Do you remember being asked what you wanted to be when you grew up?

....

Well, now that we are older and hopefully a bit wiser, it might serve us well to take pause to reflect upon our own childhood fascinations. Perhaps there was something essentially important, a furtive clue embedded within them, designed to guide us into adulthood with a purpose of its very own. Perhaps there was something there that called out to us, letting us know exactly what we wanted to do.

So now I ask, what did you want to be when you grew up? Was it a doctor or a fireman, a pilot or ballerina? Were you going to be a mom or a teacher, a veterinarian or musician? Whatever it was that you wanted to become, that innate desire was inspired by a soulful feeling inside of you, a feeling that excited you and somehow just felt *right*. You didn't have to think long and hard about it; it was something you instinctively just *knew*. Maybe there was something about becoming an astronomer or a nurse that called out to you. Whatever it was, it spoke to you in a way that made you feel happy, joyful, and enthused. So, what was it for you? Can you think back to when you were small and recall what it was that you loved to do?

Take a little time now, to let these thoughts dance within your being. It might prove to be useful, as you begin to explore what feels meaningful to you now.

As adults, we reflect on the origin of this internal *knowing*. We question its authenticity because we no longer seem to trust our instincts. We attempt to reason that because someone close to us was a carpenter, or multiple generations within our family have all worked their hands in wood, that this is indisputable evidence why we, too, should desire to build houses or make furniture. But tell me, how would that explain the child who wants to become a neuroscientist, whose parents know nothing of neurology or even human anatomy? Why, from within a family of lawyers, would a child want to become a wheat farmer and work the land? From where do these seemingly anomalous ideas originate? Environment and biology alone simply cannot offer us a convincingly valuable explanation.

Did it ever occur to you that within those original childhood desires resided a blueprint for what you were *meant* to do with your life? Could there truly be something more than family genetics or environment at play here, calling out to us from some unforeseen origin? Could we truly have been responding to an inner Calling, beckoning to guide us within our lives? It is very important for us to think on these things, as our reflections might offer us important insight into an agreement we made before taking the Leap, but can no longer recall.

A Different Path

But what if from the time that you were small, your life didn't unfold in this way? What if, instead, your life was plagued by poverty or trauma and you didn't have the luxury of living in a safe environment, feeling loved and cared for? If you were a child who suffered ongoing illness, never having the opportunity to enjoy dreamy thoughts and simple childhood pleasures, could you still have experienced an inner sense that you were meant to do something very special in your life?

It is a fact that an overabundance of trauma and angst occurring at a tender age can damage a developing heart and mind, leaving little room for that young child's imagination to roam freely. If you were born into poverty or lived with a disabling illness, if you were a child of violence or had no stable family to call your own, then it is highly possible that you lost touch early on with that internal spark, that Genius that was born within you. It may be that you were simply too busy trying to survive within a world that held no regard for your sweet, tender soul.

While this is appallingly possible, it is likely, though, that somewhere within you, there is a place that has safeguarded this feeling, and now it must be carefully coaxed out into the open so that it may become refreshed and renewed. You just need to discover the steps on your path that will lead you to knowing how to do this and embrace your willingness and desire to do so.

Forgetting Our Plan

It could be, though, that you have simply forgotten what it was that you enjoyed when you were small. Sometimes life has a way of blurring our vision and dimming our memories to those delicately poignant moments, cast to serve as glimpses into our possible future selves. But why would this be?

There are numerous causes for this type of forgetting, an escape from remembering, which often leaves us feeling abandoned and unsafe within our personal world, without our understanding why. Burdened by too much trauma, we might easily fail to see those prescient hints of our innate Genius, leaving us with a falsified and empty impression that life is nothing more than a dull series of random occurrences, strung together in some strange and discordant continuum. And from within this discord and sense of mediocrity, a debilitating urgency may have reared its ugly head, directing you to grasp after whatever offered you the illusion of pleasure, not knowing when something "good" might pass your way again.

Regardless of the reason, if we have no idea of what we truly love to do, and if we do not experience any sense of personal meaning and value within our lives, this has the capacity to become the causative agent for aberrant behaviors and debilitating addictions. Unfortunately, this problem then becomes exacerbated by the circularity of its nature. When we are occupied by unhealthy habits and behaviors, this in turn shields us from any awareness of the existence of inner directive or internalized Calling, leaving us feeling empty and alone, not knowing how to move forward.

When we come to grasp this understanding, it becomes easier to comprehend how negative emotions of jealousy and competition can become a directing force for us. How can we love when we cannot trust the direction of life itself? Feeling abandoned and lacking in clear guidance, it is as though we were set adrift in a vast ocean with no sail, no rudder, no compass. Feeling lost, there is a yearning that begins to fester within us, a longing for the joy that we have missed out on and fear we will never know, and though we may not even be consciously aware of this, we sense it deeply, all the same.

Our Birthright

Combine all these feelings into one small child and multiply that by several billion people, and we have the makings for a world that is lacking the glorious luster of exuberant joy and love that by design is humanity's birthright. Sadly, there is a pervasive deficiency of faith and an overwhelming feeling of doubt blanketing our world within a smoky haze of mediocrity, and this is just not how it is supposed to be.

And so I ask, are we humans really like dandelion puffs drifting haphazardly in the wind, having no specific thought as to where we want to go or what we might like to do? Or are we, as a people, more inventive than that, creators of our own lot in life, attuned to some greater inner directive?

4.

The Purpose of Life

For all millennia that humans have inhabited this Earth, there is one compelling question that mankind returns to, again and again, in our search for deeper meaning and greater understanding. At first glance, this question may appear to be strikingly simple, but do not underestimate the power of simplicity. The spectrum of responses are oft times complicated, and most certainly, mystifying. To lightheartedly pose this question bears no great significance, but when we utter these words as our prayer to know truth, this is an act of the highest nature. And when we hear our inmost answer whispered within our own heart, we may find ourselves wandering in that middle ground: in a place where the old ways no longer work for us, yet we cannot see our pathway into the future.

So, what is this question that carries such import? What is it that we truly want to know? From within times of great brilliance or moments of dire distress, many of us have cried out, in joy and in pain, "Why am I here? What is the purpose of *my life*?"

There is a longing for understanding, a yearning to experience personal meaning and significance within our human lives. Many of us sense that we were born for something greater, but we have no idea what that might be. We wonder what life actually is, as we question its ultimate and essential purpose. Yes, we have an understanding of the biology and genetics involved with the creation of a new human being, but what is it that makes us the thinking, emoting, creative person that we are? What is it in us, that makes us, *us*?

From within times of great brilliance or moments of dire distress, many of us have cried out, in joy and in pain, "Why am I here? What is the purpose of my life?"

As a young girl, I wanted to know why I couldn't simply slip into being another person, so that I could understand what they saw, felt, and thought. The idea of being able to experience the world from someone else's internal perspective intrigued me. I remember sitting in our family kitchen one Saturday morning with one of my best friends, playfully talking about what it was that made her be her and what made me be me. I proposed to Cindy that we try to merge, one consciousness into the other, just for fun. As we sat facing each other, trying hard not to laugh, we concentrated with all our might, attempting to send messages back and forth between us. We did this for a while, each taking our turn, but how disappointing it was that nothing seemed to happen at all. Quite clearly, at the end of our little session, Cindy was still Cindy, and I was still me. Soon after, in walked my dad and some of his tennis buddies and I earnestly turned my questions to them. What might you imagine was their response to my youthful inquiry? To this day, their bewildered facial expressions are more memorable than anything they may have said at the time. Who thinks of such things on a sunny Saturday morning, when fresh coffee is brewing and the tennis was great?

Historically, we have looked to religion and philosophy in our quest for understanding, but far too often, we have been left feeling frustrated and dissatisfied, told that life is, quite simply, a *mystery*! We ask if we are our bodies or our thinking minds, and we wonder at this mystery which challenges concrete description and defies rational, linear thinking. We hear words like "soul" and "inner self" tossed about interchangeably, and we question if there is something greater to this life than our daily routines that keep us so frantically busy. We are immersed in the rhythm of the *have-tos* and *need-tos*, which only seem to deepen our collective struggles, leaving us wondering if there really is such a thing as inner peace.

Yes, our pursuit of truth is challenging, requiring us to be willing to think and respond in new and fresh ways, to be ready to break away from the pack mentality of thought. And so when we question what the purpose of life might actually be, we are treading into wild territory where we must be alert and bold and prepare ourselves to take the journey of a lifetime. And it is when we begin this journey and Leap into our quest for understanding that we might discover that our Tale of Possibility and Calling is not just a story after all, and that we, ourselves, are the master designers of our own beautiful plan: a plan we have likely forgotten altogether!

Turning Point

Just what it is that brings us to the point in our lives that we begin to reflect on these things? Some of us may have been slapped by divorce or death or some other life-altering event, while others of us have been running at a dizzying pace for far too long, without any sense of satisfaction or fulfillment to be enjoyed. So, it is highly understandable that we might come to wonder if this is all there is to life. On the other hand, maybe it doesn't have to be anything specific that happens to us at all. It is possible, instead, that we have just always had a persistent feeling within us that there was something that we were born to do, if only we knew what that was.

Over the years, I have been friends with a woman who is truly one of the kindest people I have ever met. Sarah had always been remarkably generous, volunteering her time and energy to help others make their projects come to fruition. Year after year, she chaired community committees, helped out in her kids' classrooms, and worked full-time, managing a small medical office. And year after year, Sarah would say to me, "When the kids are grown, I am going to figure out what I really want to do with my life." It wasn't that she didn't love being a mother, she just always felt that there was something else calling out to her, but she had no idea what it could be. When the time eventually arrived for her youngest child to leave for college, Sarah began to experience an unsettling emptiness building up inside her. No longer was she running at lightning speed, taking care of everyone else's needs. Instead, she found herself in the midst of an unfamiliar calm, wondering what she was going to do to fill in this gap.

While on the surface, this has the appearance of being a case of Empty Nest Syndrome, it really goes beyond that. Of course when our children leave home, there is both a physical and emotional gap left behind, but what we might not realize is that from within that open space, we have the opportunity to take pause and re-evaluate how we would like to move forward into this next phase of our lives. The problem is, though, that so many of us have no idea how to do that. When we are so busy running, tending to everyone else's needs, we are likely not giving much attention to our own, so we miss important clues that can guide us into a new direction that we really should go. Amazing things happen when we become quiet and allow our inner voice to begin to speak, when we make ourselves sit calmly amidst our own discomforts, born of changes seemingly beyond our control. Sarah simply had never had the opportunity to be entirely alone, to become acquainted with her own innate interests. What Sarah needed to understand was that what may have felt like a stressful and untimely parting instead was a wonderful opportunity for both Sarah and her daughter to grow.

Within this universal query as to the purpose of life, there resides an innate awareness of our need to feel a sense of purpose, meaning, and value in how we feel and what we do. We wonder if there is more to life than continuing to tread the pathways of our daily routines that we have now worn smooth. And not surprisingly at all, many of us have found that when we lose sight of this thought, our lives have a tendency to run amuck, leaving us feeling lost, without any clear idea of what to do next.

Moving into the Leap

So, let us again return to our tale and see how it might be able to help us to answer our question, "*What is the purpose of my life?*"

According to our story, it was we, ourselves, who determined what it was we would like to do, once we were born into these little human bodies. Along with our Guide, we, as our non-physical selves, chose our talents and abilities that we would bring with us as we Leaped into our new physical lives. These were the qualities and characteristics that defined our unique Genius, serving as an internal directive that was our Calling.

When we arrived, we were determined to excel at being human and directed to express ourselves in our most creative and inspired ways. If we were called to create a painting or a musical composition, we would do it with all the joy and love that intrinsically defined us. If it was cooking that we adored, then we would stir our essential nature of love, directly into our recipes. And so it would be if we were throwing a baseball from sixty feet across home plate, then we were pitching with the focus and intention of our naturally blissful state.

When we are doing something that is truly meaningful, we feel deeply connected to our inner and outer worlds. We are excited and joyful, and our lives feel valuable. When we do something that we love, we begin to understand the deeper purpose behind what we are doing and this connects us to the purpose of life for all. When we are experiencing this sense of wholeness, then we have the capacity to share it with others, which contributes to our collective purpose for being here, as a greater humanity.

When we are doing something that is truly meaningful, we feel deeply connected to our inner and outer worlds.

Creating Essence into Form

If the overarching purpose of our lives is to create Essence into Form, just what exactly does this mean? If our desire is to "comprehend that which has no physical form, yet whose intrinsic energy is the underpinning of all that we know as substance within our physical world," as I expressed earlier on, then where do we begin in our pursuit for understanding?

Essence may be described as the mysterious, inward nature that exists, as opposed to what is accidental, phenomenal, illusory. Essence is something that exists, especially a spiritual or immaterial entity, that same non-material force at the center of all life on this Earth.

Again, Essence is that non-material force at the center of all life on this Earth. This sounds straightforward enough, but truth be told, our ability to understand "a non-material force" remains challenging and elusive. Instinctively, we feel the vibrancy of our Essence within us in a primal sort of way, but how do we describe something that we have never seen, touched, tasted, or smelled? Perhaps if we likened Essence to our planet's sun, then we humans could be compared to the sparks of light emitted from the sun's energy. So, if every flame, every spark that originated from our sun were a tiny reflection of the sun's collective whole, we too would be individuated components, representative of our own collective Essence.

Another way we might consider this is by thinking of ourselves as expressions of light. Within the theory of Wave Particle Duality within Quantum Physics, light has the capacity to manifest itself as both an individuated Particle and also as a Wave of energy. So, let us equate our human existence to that of light, where every single human being is part of the collective wave of humanity, while simultaneously being individuals living within that collective light.

Essence is that non-material force at the center of all life on this Earth.

So, if this life is the physical expression of that which we are in Essence, then we are a living consciousness, born into physical form. When we choose what it is we want to do, we are defining our unique expression by answering that Calling within us. As we engage our talents to create a life that we enjoy, we are differentiating ourselves from the Wave of Essence, as we Particulate in our own unique and beautiful way.

What Is the Purpose of My Life?

So, if the purpose of life, overall, is to create that which we are in Spirit into a physical, human expression, how does that idea actually help us discover what the specific purpose of our own lives might be? Do we awaken each day and say to ourselves, "I'm going to create Essence into Form today!"? No, of course not. But, we might decide that we are going to practice piano, or go for a five-mile run, if we are a musician or an athlete. As we set short-term goals for ourselves, we are doing the work that allows us to enjoy the long-range benefits of employing our talents. When an actor steps out onto stage, we can be certain that he or she has spent countless hours rehearsing their role in preparation for the performance they are about to give.

As we make use of our talents and abilities, we are actively enjoying our efforts of putting our creativity into motion. When we compose that song, we are expressing our unique Genius as our response to that internal Calling. It is our Calling that acts like a beacon of light for us, as if saying, "Come right this way. This is what you were born to do!" It is our Calling that serves to guide us in the direction we are meant to go, as we establish more specific goals to help us along our way.

But the goals that we set for ourselves are not the purpose of our lives; they are simply a part of our process. It is a big clue for us that when we establish specific goals and accomplish them as planned, we will likely experience a feeling of emptiness: a letdown, leaving us wondering what's next. This is a common occurrence that companions goal-setting, suggesting to us that the goal-setting is not what is ultimately important to us. Rather, it is living our specific Calling that is the true purpose for each of us, individually. And as each one of us lives our truest purpose, we are creating that which we are in our non-physical Spirit into a beautiful and very human form.

5.

Calling

There is a freshness of being that is emerging within all of us. We are being urged to Leap into that which we have long ago forgotten, yet so dearly hunger for. When we look to our childhood, it is there that we may discover the clues that will lead us to our answers. It is when we identify and embrace the things that we love to do, actively engaging them on a daily basis, that we will feel a resonance warming us from within as we begin to allow it to guide us on our way.

Living a life that we love is a highly creative act, and yet we often find it to be an elusive challenge. We try to imagine ourselves happy and joyful, our days laced with an ease and comfort in all that we do. Yet, far too often, the images we conjure up in our mind are not compatible with the actual activities and routines that we carry out each day. We need to earn livings and many of us have children to care for. We have businesses to run, classes to attend, and somewhere in there, we need to get some exercise. There is an endless list of responsibilities to fulfill and at the day's end, many of us are just too tired to think about anything else. So, how is it, we ask, that we might actually begin to create a life that we love, if we are not already living one?

In our quest for an answer, within our tale, we learned that we each had our own unique Genius and a mission to craft a life that we would love, using that brilliance. This was the point: to enjoy our gifts and the creative process of creating a life that would hold meaning and value for us. But once we had arrived, we discovered there were other pushes and pulls pressuring us, leaving many of us utterly unaware that we were ever Called to do anything specific at all! And so we ask, just what is this Calling, and if we truly have one, what might that be?

And so we ask, just what is this Calling, and if we truly have one, what might that be?

When I was young, I often wondered what it was that ignited me to become awash in a symphony of sheer inspiration, compelling me to compose music and write poetry. What was it that thrilled me with the vibrations of my singing voice, and from what magical portal did my intense desire to play piano emerge, while only three years old? I wanted to know why I loved to put my hands into dirt, potting African violets or planting trees, and what was it that fascinated me about watching them grow. From where did these inner urgings originate? What was their truest source?

Calling is an internal directive of pre-encoded information, much like the messages carried within our DNA, designed to activate a compelling desire within us, leading us to express ourselves in our own unique way. Calling is that which reflects our intrinsic passions, serving to define our own unique nature and how we present ourselves within our world. When we feel a driving force that directs us to climb a mountain or gaze into a microscope, this is the gift of Calling, whispering in our ear. It is Calling that lights the way for us to discover our beautiful Genius, waiting to be tapped and brought out into the light of day.

When people are young, most often, they know what they love to do. Some feel the pull to become doctors, parents, or computer programmers, while others are inspired to be artists, tour guides, or business leaders. Sometimes, though, things happen in life that are not at all part of our childhood dreams, and we find ourselves traveling down alternate life pathways than those we had originally imagined. We all know that life can become complicated quickly and not necessarily of our own design, causing us to take pause and wonder, *Is this all there is*? And if we should find ourselves asking aloud, "What do I want to be when I grow up?" it's a dead giveaway that we are searching for something to make our lives feel meaningful, but we just don't know where to begin.

When we are in search of Calling, we are looking for a portal to appear: a doorway to open or a light to shine brightly, beckoning for us to boldly step into that luminescence and walk on through, into the practice of doing what it is we love to do within our daily lives. It is when we finally yield to this understanding, becoming attentive to answering our Call, that our lives will actually become a richly woven tapestry of our very own creation, as we resonantly fulfill our destiny, our true purpose for living.

6.

Genius

I have often tried to imagine what our world would be like if each one of us became acutely aware of what we are impassioned by. To draw upon a very simple remembrance of something that served to excite us when we were young is a reflective journey we all should take. Most assuredly, if we allowed ourselves the luxury of time for such contemplation, we would come to understand that each one of us has our own unique Genius that calls out to us, and according to our tale, it is a Genius that we carefully selected for ourselves, along with the help of our Guide.

Truly, the possibilities of what we can do are limitless, within our collective whole of humanity, but individually, each one of us has more defined, specialized abilities that we simply must not ignore. It is a fact that when we embrace our gifts, we feel joyously fulfilled and inspired to awaken to each day. But, when we are off-track, living a life not crafted of our own accord, our days become strained and problems seem to arise, without the complement of joy and inspiration to balance things out. It is when we experience a sense that something is missing, that this becomes our clue. It is then that we must begin our search and watch for that beacon of light, flashing its command for us to "Pay attention! Come this way!"

It is essential for us to find that which excites us and inspires us. We wonder, could it possibly be true that we are talented and don't even know it, that we have a unique Genius residing within? How many of us have ever actually thought of ourselves in this way? Isn't a genius someone more like Albert Einstein, who discovered the theory of relativity, a theory too complex for us non-scientific people to understand? What of Leonardo da Vinci, a brilliant Renaissance man, and perhaps the most creatively diversified person to ever have lived? These two men are examples of Genius, most assuredly, so why would we ever think of ourselves as part of this elite group of people?

We wonder, could it possibly be true that we are talented and don't even know it, that we have a unique Genius residing within?

Our perceptions define how we experience our lives, and if we hold on tightly to the idea that it is impossible for each one of us to be a brilliant talent, we will never allow enough room within ourselves to alter this possibility to actually exist. So, let's open this up and develop a greater understanding of what Genius might actually mean.

If we accept the idea that Genius can be defined by a quantitative number compiled from a series of tests created by other human beings, then we are complying with a standardization that is highly confining and is oft times considered culturally biased. If we are to understand that Genius is our unique expression of that which we are in Essence, then we must certainly abandon all attempts to define Genius as a measurement of our intellectual capacity. This simply makes no sense at all. Quite clearly, our Genius is far more expansive than that.

The word Genius is related to the Latin verb *gigno, genui, genitus*, which means to bring into being, to create or produce. But over the centuries, the idea of Genius took on another complexion of meaning, coming to be thought of as one's personal inspiration or talent. During ancient Roman times, "genii," the plural form of Genius, was defined as the guiding spirit for a person, their tutelary or personal deity. One's Genius was also known as their Daimon, or their Guide, who was thought to accompany the individual from birth to death, companioning them on the creative pathway within their physical, human lives. Does this sound at all familiar? Of course, we can't help but be reminded of our Guide in our very own tale, whose job it is to help facilitate seemingly serendipitous occurrences on our behalf, aiding us to be better able to tap into our own unique talents and abilities.

Within the creative arts, it is not uncommon for an artist to joyfully voice that they have been visited by their Muse. It is an expression that reflects an experience of a particularly attuned time of creative flow, feeling as though their Genius had just tapped them on the shoulder and offered up their prize. Others hypothesize that one's Genius can be expressed in a variety of forms, sometimes referred to as multiple intelligences. In 1983, Howard Gardner, a professor at Harvard University, published his book, *Frames of Mind*, wherein he describes there to be seven types of intelligences, each representing its own form of Genius. Gardner believed that every person has their own unique learning style and once they have discovered what that is, whether it be spatial, musical, interpersonal, intrapersonal, linguistic, bodily/kinesthetic, or logical/mathematical, that within the framework each individual is instinctively drawn to, they are able to learn and express themselves in a highly inspired way. Other theories propose that Genius is a result of heredity, but as we conceptually discussed in an earlier chapter, we wonder how a child prodigy classical pianist could possibly be nothing more than the genetic expression of five generations of farmers preceding him.

Yes, there are many contrasting theories describing the nature of Genius, but there is one idea that seems to be laced throughout them all, and it is this: When we become deeply pulled to something we love to do, we are experiencing a very strong, intuitive knowledge about our areas of significant interest, leading us to consistently express ourselves in highly passionate and original ways. This is the way of Genius. It is when we deepen our interest and actions that we are Octaving our experience, expanding its joyful reach within us, much like the musical notes on a piano keyboard. And when we respond to this internal Calling to do what we love, we are truly tapping in to our own creative Genius, in attunement with our own life's mission.

While some of us may have experienced the exuberance of doing things we adored to do when we were children, it is important to note that not all passions are born within our youth. Some may wait until later on in life to reveal their gifts to us. This does not preclude that the "writing may have been on the wall" early on, so to speak. Oft times the child who adored building with blocks, drawing, and doing jigsaw puzzles later discovers his passion to become an architect. It could be that the child who loved communicating with others and thrived within group learning environments would in adulthood become an entrepreneurial leader with a passion to create and run their own company.

While it is possible for the Genius within each of us to have been damaged by a controlling and confining environment when we were very young, the creative spirit within us never dies. It is my enduring feeling that it is never too late to uncover our passions and to embrace that intrinsic Genius that resides in every one of us. Whether we realized our gifts when we were children or still have little idea what they might be, there is no doubt that there is a beautiful Genius residing within each one of us. If we, indeed, created our own life plan, it should come as no surprise that along with our Guide, we cleverly left a trail of clues for ourselves to find our way back to that which we loved.

....

It is my enduring feeling that it is never too late to uncover our passions and to embrace that intrinsic Genius that resides in every one of us.

....

Now, all we need to do is find out what that might be.

7.

Octaving and Streaming

When we speak of doing things that we want to do, we are usually only intermittently focused on these pleasures, fitting them into our lives, as we are able to find the time. These are often simple activities that bring a little joy into our days. It could be that we might go out into the garden and cut blossoms for our home or decide to take a long walk around the lake. Maybe it is playing a round of golf that makes us happy, or going out for a lazy lunch on a Sunday afternoon. Whatever it is that gives us a lift, these activities contribute to creating a sense of well-being and balance in our lives.

....

Whatever it is that gives us a lift, these activities contribute to creating a sense of well-being and balance in our lives.

....

But when we find something that strongly captures our attention and we return to it over and over again, this is a clue, a prescient hint that we are rubbing shoulders with something that bears significant meaning and value for us. When we find ourselves driven by an internal urging and simply can't stay away, this is the point where we begin to deepen, or Octave within our experience, taking it to another level of intention within us.

Octaving—Deepening the Joy

I knew a woman who loved to knit. During the evenings after dinner, she and her husband enjoyed watching television together, relaxing after a long day's work. Night after night, they would retire to the family room, and Elizabeth would pull out her basket of knitting as her husband turned on the TV. She loved the feel of the yarn in her hands and relaxed into the rhythmic motion of the needles. After a time, it became clearly apparent that she wasn't attentive to the programs they were watching, but rather, she felt herself slipping into a calm and quiet place within herself, where she felt a beautiful sense of peace and happiness. As Elizabeth knit, she was imagining how lovely it might be to meet other women who also loved to knit, sharing their stories and their passion for their art, wrapped in a circle of love. Quite remarkably, after enough long nights of knitting and dreaming, Elizabeth went online, and indeed, began connecting with other women who were also interested in sharing their love for knitting. Together, they formed a group of knitters who met once a week to share their craft, with the focus on donating their works to elderly people who couldn't afford warm sweaters.

Octaving allows us to connect with our spiritual Essence as we create that energy into a freshly beautiful physical form.

What a wonderful example of a woman taking a hobby she enjoyed and Octaving her experience, creating a beautiful opportunity to fulfill a deep desire to connect with like-minded women and to generously share their gifts with others. When we move from the occasional, superficial interest to a dedicated, passionate engagement, we are deepening our response as we answer the Call to express our own unique Genius in our own creative way. Octaving allows us to connect with our spiritual Essence as we create that energy into a freshly beautiful physical form.

Streaming

Octaving can also be an entirely spontaneous occurrence, much like the Expansion I experienced as a young girl while lying in my bed at night. Octaving is a bridge between our creative inspirations and our body chemistry, as we begin to open up to our intrinsic Genius and feel the creative joy Streaming into our beings. When we focus and become fully engaged in what we are doing, our conscious awareness begins to flow, allowing us to lose all awareness of time and external activities going on around us. This is when we begin to Stream. Instead of being present in our outer world, we are attuning ourselves to the brilliance of our creative Essence and welcoming it to travel freely within us, Streaming the energy of passion and inspiration within our beings. It is here that our Genius resides and becomes ignited, and we need to tenderly care for its well-being. When we care for our Genius, we will experience a joy that defines our purpose for living, encouraging us to develop our ability to sustain this level of being and to Stream with it in all that we do.

8.

Creativity

Every human being is born with unique gifts, with beautifully original and creative talents. We know from The Leap that along with our Guide, we selected our specific interests and determined how we would like to use them once we were here. Yet, however true this may be, far too many of us have never thought of ourselves as being creatively inspired.

"Me? A creative person? Why, I don't have a creative bone in my body!"

Knowing that many people feel this way, it is very likely that we don't really understand just what being a creative person means. We may have a limiting and outdated idea that precludes all possibility of our being included within this exclusive club. Truly, creativity is the essential expression within each one of us, designed to inspire us to keep moving along our path. While we commonly think of creativity as being the ability to cause something entirely unique to come into existence, it is also the ability to transcend conventionally accepted ideas and to generate meaningful new ways of expressing our interpretations of those things that already exist. Even the greatest of all artistic masters looked to their predecessors and peers for ideas and inspiration. While some may say that there is nothing created that is ever entirely new, we most certainly do have the capacity to put our own original signature on a thing, offering a vibrant and fresh perspective that most certainly will inspire.

Creativity can be expressed in an infinite number of ways, from within almost any situation we find ourselves. Life is a highly creative act and it is simply ours to discover what it is that we want to create. Think of the artist Andy Warhol, who produced the Campbell Soup Collection, which became an iconic success in 1962. Warhol took a commonplace household item and painted a series of thirty-two canvases, each one being a variety of soup the company offered at the time. With this transformation of the commonplace into his artistic vision, Warhol ushered in a brilliant pop cultural art movement that has successfully endured for the last fifty years.

....

Life is a highly creative act and it is simply ours to discover what it is that we want to create.

....

Creativity also resides within the field of athletics. What of the athlete who has the ability to adapt and respond spontaneously to whatever situation might develop within a game? This ability to adjust to any circumstance almost instantaneously is an essential and creative act within any sport. Think of the baseball player who intuitively knows in which direction and at what velocity the baseball will travel, simply from "reading" the ball off the crack of the bat. What is the source of this insight, to be able to respond in less than a second, to run left or right, or to leap through the air to make that breathtaking catch?

There is a beautiful magic about creativity that generates a very high feeling within us, a feeling that we desire to experience as often as we can. There is no doubt that it is this heightened awareness that motivates us to continue with our activity of choice, constantly searching for ways to make it even more interesting as we go along. Though it may seem obvious, it is relevant to note that there is a direct relationship between our intrinsic, creative abilities and what we actually love to do. It makes sense that the artist/painter loves to paint, the musician needs to compose or play her instruments, the athlete must run and leap, and the leader must speak out and motivate people. It also stands to reason that the more often we engage in our particular "art form," the better and more talented we become, which serves to yet increase our level of attention and fascination with what we are doing, while deepening our connection to that which Calls out to us.

It is important for us to understand that every single thing we do is a creative act: how we speak, the thoughts we think, the way we love, and how we perceive the world we live in. There is nothing that we engage in that is not part of our creative expression, when we are consciously living and not yielding to some outside directive. As creative beings, our purpose for living is to express our natural Essence within our physical lives, through our creative talents, our unique Genius. Interestingly enough, there are as many ways of being creative as there are people on this planet, and it is our job to identify what it is that Calls out to us and to tap into our own creative spirit.

The Emancipation of a Stick-Figure Artist

When I was a little girl, I was always drawn to art, but once we arrived at the art studio at my elementary school, I had no idea where to begin and just felt completely lost. My teacher would give us a project to do, but never offered any instruction that actually helped me to do it. I was strictly a stick-figure "artist" and felt frustrated when I picked up a pencil to draw, feeling so limited and talentless, and somehow it just didn't feel right. I wondered why I couldn't draw something that looked like what I had intended it to be. I wanted my people to have bodies and heads that actually resembled a real person and longed to feel my own creative idea flowing into my mind, so that I could create something beautiful and unique on paper. But as hard as I tried, my artwork never changed. I just figured I wasn't an artist and never would be.

Fast forward thirty years to when I was invited to attend a very small, private drawing class. I still had this desire in me to be able to draw, though I had never experienced a moment's satisfaction with my attempts. I accompanied my friend, and together we listened as the teacher spoke of learning how to "see." She told us that our human minds had a powerful way of limiting our ability to interpret what we were viewing, and that it was we, ourselves, that were keeping us from being able to actually draw what we were looking at.

Through a series of interesting techniques taken from the book *Drawing on the Right Side of the Brain*, she guided us to invert the object we were going to draw and then to simply look at the lines and duplicate them on our paper. I happened to be looking at a chair that she had, indeed, placed upside down, with the intention that my mind no longer identify it as a chair but rather see the relationship of the structure within the chair and how the lines interfaced with one another. I lifted my pencil and began to draw what I was seeing, and when she told us to stop and rotate our paper upside down, I was absolutely stunned. Where it never had been possible before, I had drawn this object with dimension and perspective and it looked exactly like what it was. I had, in fact, drawn a chair.

I was very excited as we continued to engage in more exercises similar to this one, and that night when I went home I never went to sleep. Everywhere I turned, I saw something in my home that I wanted to draw, and as the night flew by I had page after page of sketches of things that looked like what I had intended for them to be. I was astounded. I had discovered that we do not need to learn how to draw, but rather, in order to draw, we need to learn how to see.

I had discovered that we do not need to learn how to draw, but rather, in order to draw, we need to learn how to see.

A mental shift must occur, away from a verbal, analytical approach toward a more visual, perceptual way of integrating and processing what we are actually looking at. You see, when we think in words, numbers, and other symbols, we are often conceptualizing in a sequence, but not so when learning to identify what we are seeing. It is a beautifully transformative experience, where we simultaneously take in the relationships of the individual components and integrate them into a larger whole.

When we learn to make this shift within ourselves, we open up our creative pathways, allowing our energy to flow into us and Stream in an expansive and fluid way. No longer are we holding the pencil tightly, trying to draw a specific idea of a face, but rather our fingers relax and we can see the gentle curve of the jawline and how it connects to the ear. We can see that our lips are set above the indent of our chin and how the nose is settled in above the soft channel rising up from the lip. When we begin to see relationships within our art, that is when we open up to the creative flow within us and begin to tap into our Genius.

Two very important ideas emerged from within all this that I needed to understand. I had to learn to trust my inner feeling that I was meant to be an artist with the ability to draw and feel excited by what I produced, despite the fact that for most of my life I was entirely incapable of doing so. If that incapacitating feeling had survived that long, I needed to grasp the fact that there was something powerful Calling out to me, even though I didn't know how to respond. The second thing that served to complete this puzzle was that I needed to experience how to open up my being to the *possibility* of something being able to occur, enough so that I could see the relationships within the physicality of life and how they all worked together. It was essential for me to fully understand that all of life is in concert with everything else, both in the physical and the non-physical, and that the possibility and promise of life are more far-reaching than what our limited, linear minds have the capacity to perceive.

This entire experience served to confirm for me that in my desire to do my art, I was learning how to be a part of the most important relationship of all, by expressing my truest spiritual Essence into a uniquely interpreted form. I was learning how to be the Me that I was born to be.

9.

Framework, Resistance, and Mediocrity

In our quest to live a life that we really love, we are often met by a resistance created by the very environment we are born into. Within our families and communities exists a defining structure of beliefs and traditions that has served as the guiding light for how we are supposed to live a good life. The problem is that the ideas and practices embraced over the expanse of many generations no longer reflect what the current rhythms of life call for. Instead of feeling supported and encouraged to be our most creative, exuberant selves, we often feel stifled by these outdated guidelines, thwarted from developing into the brilliant, creative beings we so naturally are.

Imagine the young man whose father has groomed him to become a part of the family business, when all he has ever wanted is to be a park ranger and live out in the Arctic tundra, photographing wolves. How do you think he feels each day as he dons suit, tie, and briefcase, running from one corporate meeting to the next?

When we are born, we Leap into families that are part of an already established social structure that over the decades has developed a rhythmic heartbeat of its very own. If we were to place our finger on the pulse of contemporary society, we would surely discover that many of these old rules no longer apply, no matter how much they still dominate culturally. When we Leaped, we came in with our own ideas, desires, and needs that perhaps did not fit within the confines of what was expected of us. Within our Tale, we were advised that we might forget in entirety that we had created our own plan, leaving us vulnerable to the persuasions of the family story lines of the lives we were leaping into. So how can we create a change within ourselves and within our world that allows us to live a life we love, without yielding to the pressures and standards that do not work for us at all?

Perhaps if we come to understand the nature of resistance, it might assist us in creating new pathways that will lead us in the direction we desire. It is important for us to fully grasp the fact that this is entirely doable, but first we need to loosen the grip of old behaviors and ideas that serve to keep us in a holding pattern that we now need to disrupt.

When we live a life of meaning, this creates a sense of joy, happiness, and pleasure. At a very simple level, doing activities that are fun makes us feel happy and light, and that's great. But when we tap into those things that Call to us and begin to do them, this deepens our happy feelings and we experience a dynamic energy that drives us into a more resonant joy. We tap into the collective Wave of energy, the Essence of everything that physically exists, and we begin to expand.

....

When we live a life of meaning, this creates a sense of joy, happiness, and pleasure.

....

When we deepen and touch into our Essence, we begin to create, as we shift into a place of Streaming. And when we shift our attention and perspective and begin doing things that make us feel really good, we are able to push back against the prescribed framework, and create our own joyful way of being.

But the longer we stray away from that which we love to do, the more our lives take on a manner of mediocrity, leaving us feeling uninspired and flat. Our days become cycles of repetition, which invariably lead to gnawing pain and the temptation to engage in aberrant and self-destructive behaviors, if only to feel *something,* to spice things up and feel alive, when all they really succeed in doing is tearing our lives down. Mediocrity is insidious and deadly, lulling us into a dull place where we resist responding to our Calling, simply because it seems too hard to do anything about it. When we are caught up in the malaise of not-doing, altering the familiar patterns seems to require too much effort. When we live within the confines of mediocrity for too long, we begin to resist doing something other, resist doing anything at all, that could give us a lift back into ourselves, back to where we were when we Leaped into these lives in the first place. It is this malaise and mediocrity from which we'll be breaking free through the process I outline in Part Two.

10.

When We Don't Do What We Love

From the age of twelve, all Edward ever dreamed of was recording and performing his music, traveling around the world and making people happy. As a young boy, he taught himself to play guitar, and soon his lead electric guitar riffs became pure genius. When he and his bands would perform, Edward was always front and center: the lead singer, lead guitarist, the guy who all the girls swooned for. Bright lights and city stages called out to him. When he finished college, he set out on the road to tour. Over the next few years, he and his band worked hard, slept little, and money was hard to come by. He loved the creative process, but soon after their engagement, his bride-to-be, Cynthia, began leaving hints that perhaps it was time for them to settle down and for him to get a job that paid well. After all, wasn't it time that they begin to think about their future, so they could start to move forward with having a family and creating a real home? Edward was torn, as he was doing what he truly loved, and yet he adored his fiancée, who wanted them to walk a different path together, a prescribed route meant to prepare them for a life of marital bliss, comfort, and security.

Of course, this is a classic story of juxtaposing the pull to live one's life as one is Called to do, in contrast to growing into the responsibilities of adulthood, where the have-tos and must-dos become the driving force behind our actions. As we moved twenty years into the future, Edward had continued to work hard and care for his family throughout the years, but his passion for music had long since been abandoned. Then came the day when Edward received notice that his job had just been terminated, and he felt a panic rising up inside of him. Of course he knew he needed to look for a new job, and soon after began his search, but after several months of looking for work, Edward became deeply depressed. Very worried about her husband, Cynthia thought a little fun might help and suggested they go out to a local restaurant to listen to some music, hoping it might perk him up. Reluctantly, he agreed, and off they went.

By the end of the first song, Edward's chest had tightened into a knot as a flood of longing rushed through him, bringing him back to the days when he used to perform. He remembered the feel of the guitar strings on his fingers and the sound of his own voice singing out through the PA. He missed the easy life that he had loved so much, now nothing more than a distant dream, long ago forgotten. Just what was he supposed to do with all this? How was he supposed to deal with the aching in his heart?

After watching her husband all night, Cynthia saw how much he still loved music and realized that perhaps this could be a key to helping him become the happy, creative man she had married. Although money was tight, the next day she went out and purchased a guitar, leaving it on their bed for Edward to find. Later, when Edward came home from looking for work, he went upstairs and she held her breath. Endless time seemed to pass as she waited patiently, hoping to hear the strumming of the guitar and his voice singing out. And just when she thought she could wait no longer, she heard the first sweet chord he played, and her heart rolled over in her chest. Upstairs, Edward's eyes shined brightly, as the thrill of playing began to flush his face and warm his fingers into action for the first time in twenty years.

Edward played every single day, and as the weeks passed, his heart became lighter, as he brainstormed new ideas of what he could do for work. After much deliberation, he decided to try teaching guitar lessons to kids, hoping they might love learning their instrument. As Edward continued to play his guitar, more and more students were signing up, and soon he had a full roster of students. After a time, Edward was living his passion for music, having found a way to care for his family reasonably well, while feeling deeply soul satisfied and inspired within himself. Truly, it was a beautiful thing. Thankfully, Edward's wife had attuned herself to a solution, even though she had only thought of it as a temporary fix. Oft times, these things actually work in this way. We are given one step and then another, until we are on a pathway that feels right and good.

Of course, though, not all stories have such happy endings. When we don't do what we love to do, our lives have a way of running off-course and we miss the cues and taps on the shoulder that are meant to help us find our way. We forget that we have Guides who are trying to help us, and instead, we turn a deaf ear.

When we don't do what we love to do, our lives have a way of running off-course and we miss the cues and taps on the shoulder that are meant to help us find our way.

Let us think back to the young fellow who wanted to study the life patterns of tundra wolves, yet instead had gone into the family business. How many mistakes did he have to make until the family finally asked him to leave the company? A lack of interest and inadequate focus yield sloppy, compromised results. How devastating had it been for him to turn down a research grant to photograph and study those wolves in the wild? If only he had listened to that inner voice long before, he could have spared the strain and upset with his family and would have been happily doing what he truly wanted to do. Instead, he had allowed himself to be directed by his parents' expectations, rather than answering his own Call.

But life has a way of waking us up and redirecting us to where we are meant to go, hopefully sooner than later, if we are willing to listen. But if we are not willing, those bumps and taps will increase in intensity, until we are being "hit over the head," and eventually, when we have finally had enough of that, hopefully we will yield and become willing listeners to what our Guides actually have to say.

Our Creative Challenge

Our challenge begins when our creative selves are seemingly locked away beyond our own reach. When we lose sight of who we are and what we are meant to do, we miss out on living lives that we truly enjoy. Instead of feeling joyous and free, we become uncomfortable and confined within our daily living, full of anxiety and frustrations that really should not exist. We are meant to be a world of highly creative and inspired people, not a world that is traumatized and stressed into living lives that are tediously strained.

....

We are meant to be a world of highly creative and inspired people, not a world that is traumatized and stressed into living lives that are tediously strained.

....

It is when we are unable to express ourselves in some relevant and important way that aberrant behaviors are sure to surface. It stands to reason that we need to find our way back to living a life that has meaning and value, to live a life that we truly can love. If we all were able to do this, together, our world would be a very different place indeed.

11.

What We Need

We are living in a time of great transition, both within our world and within our own lives. We know that the old ways are no longer working for us, and yet we find ourselves suspended somewhere between where we once were and where we are going. There is a new way emerging, a pathway that is compelling us to awaken to that voice inside, directing us to take pause from what we are doing and become very quiet and still. We are seeking transformation from the lives we have been living with a determination to align ourselves with our truest desires, so that we may emerge from our cocoon as a vibrant expression of who we were born to become.

....

We are living in a time of great transition, both within our world and within our own lives.

....

We must gather our energies and focus on them with an intention to restore the plan that we co-created along with our Guide. Though before we take action, there must be a time for solitude, a time of reflection and preparation, where at first, we might feel a loneliness creep into our beings. But truly, this is not loneliness, but rather a response to the framework of enculturation that has driven us to live our lives at breakneck speed. Rather than feel lonely, this space allows us to become liberated from this frenetic busy-ness that has served to dominate our daily routines. We need to learn how to create the time that we don't believe we have, to do things that are enjoyable and meaningful to us. And when we have begun to focus on our "artistic" vision, we must commit to a path that is purposeful and self-directed.

There is so much more to life than simply going through the motions of our familiar daily cycles. It is about opening ourselves up to recognize what our natural talents and inclinations are and realize that we have the ability to choose what we actually want to do, with the capacity to do it.

When we learn to become present with the quiet within, a new voice will emerge: a voice that will whisper to us, our truest heart's desire. It is when we have connected with this internal awareness that we will give ourselves the opportunity to align with our Calling, to embrace our Genius and fulfill the purpose of our lives. It is our choice. What do you choose?

....

It is our choice. What do you choose?

....

PART TWO

The Alchemy of Creating a Life You Love

"Living is a form of not being sure, not knowing what next or how. The moment you know how, you begin to die a little. The artist never entirely knows. We guess. We may be wrong, but we take leap after leap in the dark."

Agnes de Mille

12.

The Process

"At the moment of commitment the entire universe conspires to assist you."

Johann Wolfgang von Goethe

Somewhere along the timeline of our lives, there are questions that we must ask ourselves, though likely, as we were growing up, many of us were never encouraged to do so. If we desire to create a life that we love, we first must begin by taking an honest look at what we have been doing and be willing to ask ourselves, "Am I genuinely happy? Am I creating time for myself to do things that I enjoy, time to think and reflect, and time to feel creative and at ease? Or am I just going through the motions of awakening each day, madly running from home to work and back again, only to get up and repeat the whole thing the very next day?"

Life was not designed to be a series of troublesome lessons or a process of simply surviving one day after the next. We were not born into these bodies only to be driven by hardship and struggle. Rather, we came here to experience the joy of expressing our creatively beautiful, spiritual Essence in all that we do. Contrary to common perception, creating a wonderful life does not require having lots of money, a big home, and a closet full of clothes. We simply need to understand that we were born with our own unique gifts, and as we embrace and express those talents and abilities, we will begin to travel on a pathway of our own design, one creatively enriched by the choices we make. It is when we decide to actively choose what it is we want to do that we will begin to live our true life's purpose, by living our Calling and sharing our beautiful Genius within our world. Yes, it is true that we all have financial concerns that need to be addressed. It is very important to have reliable means to take care of ourselves and those we are responsible for, making sure to have enough of what we truly need so that we may feel comfortable, healthy, and at ease in our lives. We all need food, clothing, and a roof over our heads. We need to be able to pay our bills and would love to be able to generate a nice savings, as well. So how, we might ask, will we find the time and energy to do something new, something we are Called to do, when we are already too busy working and taking care of what we must?

The simple answer, for the moment, is that you can, and you will learn the steps of how to do this within the following chapters. Whether you continue to earn your living with the work that you currently do or find a way to change careers as you go along, that will be your choice, but you most definitely can be actively engaged in activities that you truly enjoy and still take care of business. You see, feeling happy and fulfilled is not predicated on making vast fortunes of money or garnering towering prestige. It is about learning to balance your responsibilities with your innate desires and creating a plan that allows you to feel joyfully inspired, while doing both.

We must dare to ask ourselves if we are truly happy and be willing to take a fresh, insightful look at our lives as they are today. When we do this, we are calling in the powerful forces of our creative universe to get behind us and help us to focus on becoming the inspired beings we were born to be. As we align with the intuitive insights from our Guide and reaffirm our intentions, we can begin anew, full of the promise and possibility that companioned us as we Leaped into our physical selves. It is when we begin to slow ourselves down long enough to welcome the hush of solitude within that we will expand our capacity to attentively reflect on where we have been and where we would like to go. As we open to the true nature of our search, we must be kind and gentle with ourselves, understanding that we have done the best we can, but now it is time for us to do better. It is time to thrive, to live as we are Called to do, and no longer simply survive within the confines of an architectural framework that likely never suited us very well.

As we expand into our processes of reflection and subsequent action, we will develop the ability to clear out the clutter within our hearts and homes. We will establish healthy new ways of living in mind, body, and spirit and give ourselves the tools we need to be able to do what we love and love what we do, still able to beautifully take care of our commitments and responsibilities. When we create the time to align with our natural Essence, the alchemy of our transformation shall begin, inspiring us to become the creatively unique beings that we were born to be.

13.

It's All About You

AFFIRMATION

*Every day, I will feel productive, creative, peaceful, and
serene. I will laugh and love and allow myself to be loved. I
will enjoy external success, knowing this is a reflection of my
internal wellness, balance, and joy from doing something I
love to do, every single day. I will deeply value myself, taking
care of my mind, body, and spirit. I will believe in what I am
Called to do, and won't give up searching how best to
enjoy my Genius within.*

Self-Nurturing

If we are going to afford ourselves to live each day feeling happy
and whole, just what is it that we need to do and how are we
going to go about doing it? There are lots of things that can help
us start upon our journey, and very likely the thing we need most
is that which we are most uncomfortable with doing: taking care
of ourselves before we take care of everyone else around us. We
have been told that putting ourselves first is selfish. The implica-
tion here is that we need to be givers to others at the expense of
our own well-being. This is an outdated premise, if it ever had
any real value at all.

Selfishness is defined as being *the lacking of consideration for others, while placing emphasis on one's own pleasure or profit above all else*. If we take the time to reflect on this concept, we will see that taking care of oneself has absolutely no resemblance to this definition, whatsoever. Just as we might insist that our loved ones have time to relax and exercise, to eat well and engage in activities they enjoy, so we must prioritize these very same things for ourselves. This is not selfishness; this is self-care. We have to make this become an integrated part of our lives, an essential requirement, before we can possibly consider taking tender care of another.

Just as we might insist that our loved ones have time to relax and exercise, to eat well and engage in activities they enjoy, so we must prioritize these very same things for ourselves. This is not selfishness; this is self-care.

Perhaps we can better understand this idea by thinking of the oxygen-mask analogy. We are all familiar with the announcement made every time we strap ourselves into an airplane seat: *"Should the cabin lose pressure, oxygen masks will drop from the overhead cabin. Please place the bag over your own mouth and nose before assisting others."* When we apply this concept to our lives, in actuality, this becomes a highly selfless teaching. Simply expressed, if you lose consciousness, you will be of no help to anyone else, so put on your own mask first and then turn your attention to those around you who may need your help.

You see, if your tendency is to constantly give to others, yet neglect your own needs, then over time you will find that you feel exhausted and depleted and of little value to anyone else, never mind to yourself. It is a wonderful thing to be generous and kind, but before we can responsibly turn our attention and care to other people, we must first focus our attention on our own well-being and the importance of creating an authentic and stable environment as a platform to create our lives from. As our Tale has told us, we each have our own personal destiny to fulfill. If we are so busy taking care of everyone else's needs and desires, we will miss out on what we designed for ourselves to be doing.

We will never experience joy and the sense of fulfillment if we don't tend to our basic needs and turn our attention to living our own Calling.

I recently received a message from a woman named Taylor, who shared with me that for the first time in her adult life, she is beginning to take care of herself. She told me that for years, she had absolutely no idea of what she even liked to do because she was always too busy caring for her family to even take the time to consider the idea. Not long after her thirty-year marriage crumbled, she decided to explore some of the things she had truly enjoyed when she had been a young woman, and discovered that she loved to paint. Though Taylor works a full-time job, she decided to take art classes in the evenings. She was very excited to tell me that while she had anticipated that she would be too tired to paint, instead she discovered just the opposite. By diving into her canvas and brushes and putting on some music, Taylor found that the hours flew by and yet she hadn't even sensed the time passing.

We will never experience joy and the sense of fulfillment if we don't tend to our basic needs and turn our attention to living our own Calling. We did not take the Leap into being human with an unlimited amount of time to be here. Life is precious and passes by quickly and we must not squander the gifts we were born with. Now is the time to create a life that we desire and we need to begin by taking care of ourselves. Much like a house that has been neglected over the years and suffers from lack of attention, so it is for us when we fail to take care of ourselves in mind, body, and spirit; we, too, will suffer and begin to fall apart.

Your Voice Inside

Learning anew to create a life that you will enjoy can be difficult to do. After a lifetime of listening to the messages directed at us from the significant people we are surrounded by, for better or worse, we find those messages insidiously lodged within our psyches, rearing their ugly heads when we least need them to. Most certainly, we are all accustomed to our personally well-worn patterns, so when we attempt to change our behaviors, we can be assured that those very same messages will attempt to shout us down. With an air of authority, they will impart to us that we don't deserve to do things differently, that we are not entitled to do what we want. The message is blasted at us, loudly and clearly, that we are being selfish by tending to ourselves, that we will be letting others down, and quite simply that this is unacceptable.

The question we must ask ourselves though is this: *Unacceptable to whom*? If we are going to dare to make the changes that we desire, we need to take a hard look at what those messages that threaten to take us down might actually be.

The Negative Chatter

In their origin, these messages were projected at us by the social framework we had Leaped into, and over time, we accepted them to be truths within ourselves. For example, the message *You are not creative*, transformed into *I am not creative*, serves to keep us from acting on our talents and abilities. The following are examples of what some of those messages might be. No doubt, you can easily add your own negative chatter to this list:

I am not creative. I have no talent.

I don't deserve to be happy at the expense of my loved ones' happiness.

I won't finish the work. I can't follow through.

I am too old. I should have done this when I was younger.

I won't be able to take care of myself financially.

I am too busy. I have too much to do.

I can't take care of my family properly and do what I want to do.

I _____

fill in your own negative messages

These self-deprecating messages get handed down, parent to child, generation to generation, causing a resistance from within us to be bold enough to move in a new direction of our own choice. These are the ideas that have served as our rules and bylaws to live by, assuring that we do what we are supposed to do, when we need to do it. In accordance with our families, friends, teachers, religious leaders, and our business superiors, we have followed the rules and have kept in line, without creating any waves. Yes, we have followed form and protocol, but now it is time for all that to change.

So, what can we do to loosen the grip these nullifying directives have had on us? Is it possible to actually break away from their stranglehold and begin to move in a new direction? Yes, of course we can, but it requires us to understand that we must swim against the tide and hold strong to our desires in order to make this happen. In this process, it is imperative that we remember that we are not struggling against facts and truths. In reality, these ideas are nothing more than tainted opinions and beliefs that need to be confronted within ourselves and properly put to rest. We must nurture the beautiful person we were born to be by throwing out these misguided concepts and replace them with a healthier way of living, a way which supports our true purpose for being here, so that we may get on with the very important business of living our Calling, each and every day.

Rebecca loved playing guitar and singing, and though her parents enjoyed listening to her play, they were entirely unsupportive when she announced that she wanted to go to college to study music and eventually perform on stage. Her father told her that she should look into a career that was more predictable and didn't require a specific talent. Together, her parents told her that when she got out into the real world, she would quickly discover that only the truly talented players would ever get a chance. When Rebecca became upset, they told her that they knew what they were talking about, because they had lived in the real world and she had not.

Sadly though, what they didn't realize was that this was truly Rebecca's passion in life and they had just put a gash into the fabric of her being. Instead of studying music and trying her lot at performing, Rebecca went to school for two years and then took a job as a secretary for a local attorney. It took many years for her to quiet the negative thoughts in her head, which had clearly originated from her parents. "I am not talented enough to perform. Why would anyone want to come listen to me?" Now, though, after twelve years of not playing, her need for music was so strong that Rebecca has begun to play again, singing in her daughter's pre-school class with all the children. "I just love to play; that's all. It makes me feel happy and my daughter and her friends love for me to come into their class and sing with them.

It feels wonderful. I wish I hadn't waited so long to get back to doing this."

We need to teach ourselves to become supportive of the creative spirit that resides within us and trust that it is a positive thing to create a life that we truly enjoy. As Susan Jeffers, author of *Feel the Fear and Do It Anyway*, says, " We have been taught to believe that negative equals realistic and positive equals unrealistic," but this just isn't so. We must stop the judgment and censorship we impose upon our creative desires, before they have even had a chance to spread their wings and fly. We need to terminate the power of these internal messages that have held us captive within our own skin. Isn't it time to change all this? Isn't it time to live a life that you love?

We must stop the judgment and censorship we impose upon our creative desires, before they have even had a chance to spread their wings and fly.

AFFIRMATIONS—Your Voice Inside

For every negative comment, there is a positive counterpart that we can replace it with. I have started a list of life-affirming messages that support us and encourage us to be brave enough to step out into the world and embrace our Genius within. By taking the negative statements and turning them around, we create affirmations that help us make our way out of this holding pattern and into a more expansive way of living. It is important to make use of them every day. You can write them out and keep them with you in your wallet or post them to your mirror, refrigerator, computer screen, or bedroom door. You can keep them in a list or write them out individually. One day you might want to read them all aloud, in sequence, and on other days, you might prefer to focus on only one affirmation throughout your day. And of course, you can continue with this list and create your own.

Positive, Internalized Messages

I am talented and dedicated to discovering what those talents are.

I am creative and look forward to expressing my creative inspirations.

I deserve to be happy. This will in no way take away from my loved ones' happiness.

I will take the time to focus on doing something I enjoy. When I focus on doing this, I will follow through to completion.

I am inspired and feel youthful and excited. Age does not determine creativity.

I am able to take care of myself financially. Doing activities that I enjoy each day will make me happier and, as a result, help to enhance my financial situation.

I will take tender care of myself, knowing this is not selfish.

I am a loving and kind person and enjoy helping others, but not at the risk of hurting myself in the process.

These are affirmations that can help you begin the process of leaving behind your negative thoughts and replacing them with positive messages. It is a very bad idea to absorb other people's messages directed at you, especially if they are holding you back. These negative messages are designed to sabotage your independent spirit, which is the calling card for the purpose of your life. When you feel that you are being challenged by others' thoughts, sit down and write a few of your own. Try creating three right now:

My Affirmations

I am _____
Fill in your affirmation

I want _____
Fill in your affirmation

I deserve _____
Fill in your affirmation

Taking Care of You

Of course, there are many things that we can do to give ourselves the attention and care that we deserve. Another idea that is effective in focusing loving attention on ourselves concerns how we actually start our day. It is essentially important to begin our day in a way that makes us feel good about ourselves. Though we all have a certain number of responsibilities we need to tend to, we do have the ability to make each day be something we look forward to. How many of us awaken to an alarm clock and hit snooze several times before ever touching our toes to the floor? Does this feel like a sign that we are excited and ready to get going?

It is important to awaken feeling energized and yet peaceful. It really is a wonderful combination. If you take a little time to plan ahead, you will be giving yourself a helping hand to crafting a day that you will enjoy. By planning nice, simple things for yourself to do at the beginning, middle, and end of your day, you will be creating the opportunity to look forward to these little gifts that you have designed just for you. Let's start at the beginning.

PRACTICE—Starting Your Day

Awakening and starting your day in a positive way sets the tone for how you will feel as the day unfolds before you. How wonderful it is to breathe in and affirm gratitude first thing, reminding yourself that you are a special person who deserves to be happy!

Morning Practice

1. Set your alarm to awaken yourself twenty minutes earlier than you are accustomed to. Choose a peaceful tone for your alarm. Gently sitting up in your bed, before you stand up, softly smile—with both your face and your heart—and whisper a simple thanks for the day that lies ahead of you, a day that you are going to be a direct part of planning.

2. Now move to a place in your home where you love to be, a place that makes you feel safe and happy and where you will not be interrupted for the next fifteen minutes. If you desire to practice from your bed, that is fine, too, as long as you don't fall back to sleep! It is very important to create an environment that is visually appealing to you, even if it's just a comfy chair in a corner of a favorite room. You may enjoy having some of your favorite things surrounding you, like flowers or decorative objects, for the purpose of making yourself feel happy and at ease.

3. Keep the lighting very soft. If you enjoy the glow of candles, light several so as to create a peaceful atmosphere. Keep your thoughts simple and still. Do not think ahead to your busy day as you experience this special time. Be very present in the moment.

4. After you have settled into a pleasing position, wearing your pajamas or other comfortable clothing, begin by taking

several deep breaths, inhaling slowly and exhaling gently. Do this until you are no longer consciously breathing in and out.

5. When your breathing has become quiet, begin with the following Affirmation:

> *I am a creative person and I have the ability to create a lovely day for myself, each and every day. This is my desire. This is my action.*

At first you may read the affirmation aloud to yourself, or simply memorize it ahead of time; whichever works best for you. What matters is that you focus on its meaning and its intent. Feel the strength behind the words as you speak them aloud. Feel the possibility and promise of actually creating what you desire, today and every day.

6. You are now ready to anchor these thoughts into your physical body. By lying gently on a yoga mat, towel, or blanket to cushion your body, you will begin slowly inhaling and exhaling as you awaken your body by gently stretching your arms and legs, softly rotating your neck in a circular motion and easing your back into a gentle arch and then curving it in the opposite direction. Move your body as you intuitively are drawn to do, with your awareness focused on your flow of breathing and stretching, in harmony with one another.

7. Close your eyes and still your body. Now is the time to feel the peace and beauty of the morning. Allow it to seep into you. Allow yourself to become your peace in this moment. Do this for several minutes.

8 Now, gently open your eyes and look around you. Do not think; just be. Again, smile a sweet smile and offer thanks for

the day that awaits you. When you are ready, you may get up and begin your morning routine of showering and breakfasting, while keeping the peace that is now a part of you fully engaged.

PRACTICE—Follow-Up

This Practice may be modified so that you can repeat it at noontime, even if you are not at home. You may shorten the time allotted for the practice and simply sit upright, wherever it is quiet, to do your affirmation and breathing. This will serve to reestablish your internal peace and simultaneously reinforce the idea that you have the power to create your own happiness.

AFFIRMATION FOR MIDDAY
I am a creative person and I am enjoying the process of creating my day as I desire. How I perceive my activities defines how I feel about what I am doing. I am actively engaged and feeling happy. I am my peace.

It is also a very nice way to end your day by doing something very similar to the morning practice when you have returned home, before going to bed. If you have more time, you can extend this practice to a half hour or more, whatever you desire.

AFFIRMATION FOR EVENING
I am a creative person who feels fulfilled by doing things that I enjoy and that feel meaningful. I am dedicated to creating activities within my day that bring me joy and peace.

More Thoughts for Taking Care of You

It is important to take good care of yourself in other ways, as well. The list is long, but for the moment you can begin by following through on some of these basics.

You must be sure to

- Eat well throughout your day: fresh foods, water; moderation is essential.

- Regular exercise throughout your week—best if you really enjoy what you are doing.

- Take time to relax.

- Surround yourself with things you love, that make you feel happy and inspired—for example, flowers, small treasured items, crystals, plants, or pets.

- Surround yourself with people whom you care about, and in turn, who care about you, as well.

- Before going to bed at night, turn off the television and/or stop engaging in stimulating activities an hour prior. Read something that soothes; take a bath; turn on soft lighting.

- Consider repeating the MORNING PRACTICE at noon and before retiring to bed.

- Speak lovingly and kindly to yourself.

Closing Thoughts

As we begin to craft a life that we love, we must design our own life's framework by structuring our days in our own uniquely guided way. By starting with the simple steps outlined in these Practices, we are developing our own fresh perspective, guided by our own internal actions and responses. When we begin to recognize what precious beings we actually are, we will begin to value the gift of life and the person we Leaped into this life to become.

14.

Clearing Out the Clutter

AFFIRMATION

*I will create my life with the focus of creating simplicity in all
that I do. I will not clutter my mind, my emotions, my body,
my physical environment, or my relationships. I desire to live a
simple and uncluttered life.*

Have you ever noticed how some people seem to immediately understand what they want to do with their lives, while others have no idea of what it is that they even enjoy? How many of us feel burdened with too many responsibilities and don't slow down long enough to think even one clear thought? Wouldn't it be delightful to awaken in the morning, excited and enthused, knowing you had single-mindedly arranged a day you were going to enjoy?

Unfortunately, though, for many of us, that is not how our day begins. Far too often, we are overwhelmed by all we have to do and don't really know what we might enjoy, because our lives are so filled with clutter. We have clutter in our homes, clutter in our relationships, and most importantly, our minds are cluttered with endless have-tos and to-dos that keep us running at breakneck speed. We are continually multi-tasking and bombarded by a devastating amount of information that doesn't need to be there. To make matters worse, we are forgetful and oft times overwhelmed, and we have a tedious habit of not saying "No." We are overcommitted, overextended, and overtired, leaving us little time to relax and enjoy the feel of being alone.

Alone? We have become so busy in our lives that the idea of spending time alone has taken on a peculiar feel to it. In this contemporary culture, one might ask why anyone would choose to be alone if it wasn't absolutely necessary.

Not only are our lives overly cluttered with too much to do, but our homes are filled to the brim with closets that are too full of clothes we likely haven't worn in years. Have you ever looked into your neighbor's garage, only to see it so overly stuffed that there is no room for a car? We pack our garages full of boxes and unused furniture, along with everything else we want to hide from our sight. Do we think about giving away those things we no longer use, or perhaps recycling them or tossing them out? No, we just continue to add to the clutter, as if it had no negative impact on us whatsoever.

I have a very dear friend who is one of the most fascinating people I know, but because her life had been so packed full of clutter and commitments, she never seemed to be able to follow through on her great ideas. Too many times we had all heard her say, "Once I get this house organized and have less on my schedule, I am going to sit down and write my book." Well, it seems that Elizabeth said that one too many times, and her sister, Barbara, had had enough. "Lizzie, there is never going to be a book because you just keep cramming in more and more to do and never take time to get your home and your life organized."

After cooling down from her sister's remarks, Elizabeth agreed to go through her house room by room with her sister and give away anything she didn't want or hadn't used in the last year. After a couple of months, the house was organized and Elizabeth felt a great deal more calm, but not quite calm enough. She still felt pressured with constantly having too much to do and decided to cut back on her schedule. Within a month of focusing on this, she had freed up five full days, which she used to begin her writing. The happy ending to this tale is that Elizabeth was finally doing something she had always wanted to do, but never felt she had the time or clear space to be able to do it, and now her book is nearly completed.

Of course, the flip side to this story is the fact that far too many people in our world are struggling, because they simply don't have enough. Clutter is not their problem. They are suffering from lack. They don't have people in their lives to care enough about them and they don't have enough food to eat. They are short on clothes to wear and many don't have a bed to sleep in. Yes, when we are lacking in our lives, we suffer. But the person who lives with a cluttered mind, body, and spirit is a person who is impoverished, as well. Eventually this person will become muddled and confused, without the ability to design and organize their own daily routines. They are frantically running as they wade through their jumble and can't get clear enough within their own thoughts to remember what is what they Leaped in here to do.

Has something like this ever happened to you? Have you picked up a basket of unwashed clothes and headed to put in a load of laundry, only to remember that your detergent is not in the laundry room, but instead in the kitchen where you had used it last? So you put down the basket and walk toward the door, but become distracted by the mail you had left on the table the day before. You pick up the mail and go put it into the basket to sort through later, but see a bill that you know is about to be late. You take the bill over to your computer and log in to your credit card site and pay the bill. Happy day! Your incoming emails begin to pop up in the lower corner of your laptop screen and you see a note from your best friend and have to write a quick response in return. Then you log in to your Facebook account, just for a minute, which turns into half an hour. Then the phone rings and when you answer, you become engrossed in a fifteen-minute conversation and suddenly remember that you have to get off because you have a meeting in an hour that you have to get ready for. You jump into the shower and when you get out, you realize that you don't have any towels in the bathroom to dry off with. They are in the laundry basket that is still sitting in front of the washing machine because you had gone to the kitchen to retrieve the detergent to wash the load of towels. And so it goes . . .

We are a society who doesn't know how to slow down and take time to reflect. We are sadly deficient in the personal skills we need to help ourselves learn to calm down long enough to even consider what kind of life we would like to live. We all have experienced stretches of time when we were perpetually challenged and consumed, day after day. Whether it was a project at work whose deadline loomed, or it was studying for final exams under heavy pressure, we became sleep-deprived and had no time to do anything but our work. On occasion, these things happen in life, but if we spend every single day running flat out without reprieve, we are creating a very unhealthy situation for ourselves. By combining the demands of business, family, finances, and friends, without the hope of having some degree of pleasure and ease within our days, we will, quite simply, burn out.

It is up to us to take charge and figure out a way to welcome in and discover the happiness, joy, and peace that are part of our human birthright, rather than to dwell in our unhappiness and live a life of mediocrity. Our birthright, you say? Yes, absolutely. Life is meant to be loved, and what we do and how we spend our time is truly our choice. Perhaps you think that you don't have the time or the ability to do what makes you happy, but this quite simply is not true. Do you think that if you are not a painter, a writer, or a musician that you are not a creative person?

Everything we do is a creative act. It is from within our daily living that we have the ability to consciously choose what we want to do. But if we don't, life keeps rolling along all the same, whether we like the outcome or not.

It is up to us to take charge and figure out a way to wel-come in and discover the happiness, joy, and peace that are part of our human birthright, rather than to dwell in our unhappiness and live a life of mediocrity.

If it is a compellingly interesting life that we desire, we need to be open to the possibility that we actually can do this. We must be willing to put out the effort to become consistent in our practices, accepting that this process of transformation will take a bit of time. Our social enculturation dictates that we need to be instantly gratified or we give up on our desired focus and yield to the familiar patterns already firmly lodged in place within us. The problem with this, though, is that if the old ways are not a good fit, we will remain tethered to thoughts and behaviors that have not encouraged our independence to express ourselves in our own desired ways.

So where do we begin? How do we create the simplicity that we deeply desire? How do we get rid of the clutter?

PRACTICE—Clearing Out the Clutter

Environments at Home

When your home is messy, when the laundry is piling up and the dishes are left undone, whether you realize it or not, it will have a negative impact on your well-being. Quite simply, it is very difficult to feel peaceful and focused when you are living in a cluttered mess. By working with these suggested practices, you will be able to make your way through your home, room by room, in this mission to clear out the clutter. To help yourself enjoy this process, it is a wonderful idea to play your favorite music, feeling free to sing and dance along the way!

KITCHEN—As in any room, it is best to begin with what is in our field of vision before we turn our attention to the interior of cabinets and drawers. Begin by washing the dishes and getting counters cleared of extra items that need to be put away. It is very difficult to enjoy preparing meals if every counter surface is covered with dirty dishes, pots and pans, spices, and the like. Once you have the counters cleared of all extra items, be sure to clean them well, so that they are in a fresh and healthy condition to prepare your foods on. As you have the time, it is important to clean your appliances, making sure they are in good running order. Clear out your refrigerator of old foods and wash down the interior, as well. Cabinets and drawers are next. Remove all contents, clean interior surfaces, and only return items that you will use. Give away or toss out whatever is left over.

BEDROOMS—Always begin by making the bed first. By doing this, we are creating the largest space in the room that will be instantly free of clutter, which immediately gives us a good feeling. Be sure to pick up your clothes and either put them away where they belong or place them into the basket designated for laundry to be washed. As within the kitchen, clear all surfaces of extraneous items that don't need to be there. Extra coins, jewelry, papers, and books all should have a designated place to be put away. By clearing the clutter, you will be creating an inviting retreat for you to relax and feel peaceful in. Again, if you enjoy listening to music, by all means, turn it on!

OTHER ROOMS—By following these simple steps of first clearing the visual spaces and secondarily going through closets, drawers, and cabinet interiors, eventually you will have eliminated everything that you do not find useful and you will have created a more visually peaceful environment to live in. Once you go through the initial cleaning and uncluttering phase and are experiencing the pleasure of a more Zen-like home, you can create very simple daily routines to be able to maintain what you have now accomplished.

Environments at Work/Office

As we have done at home, we must do the same in our places of business, following the same general procedures from start to finish. Additionally, be sure to put all papers into clearly labeled files so that you can be stress-free when looking for a specific document. Organizing our tools, backing up our computers, keeping a clear space to work on, all contribute to our ability to think clearly and function effectively.

LIFE ACTIVITIES—How many hours do we have in a day? The answer is obvious, but how many of us schedule in so many things that it feels as though we barely have time to sleep? It is a common occurrence in our contemporary society to frenetically run from point A to point B, with barely a moment to take a breath or stop for a proper lunch. So, what can we do to clear out the clutter of having too many activities to tend to?

LEARNING TO SAY NO—Think back to a time when someone called you up and asked you to help out with a committee or chair an event that you really didn't have time for. How did you respond? If your answer was yes, it is important to understand why you agreed to be involved. Was it something you really wanted to do, or did you agree for some other reason that really wouldn't serve you very well?

There are a variety of situations where we often have said *yes* when we wish we had said *no.* Perhaps you were asked to work late and you missed your yoga class due to your boss's lack of planning, or maybe you accepted too many social invitations and became overly stressed and then came down with a cold. Have you ever experienced the discomfort of agreeing to something that was not aligned with your personal values? There are a myriad of situations where we agree to do something that really does not contribute to our personal well-being.

Yes, we all have experienced times when, despite wishing we hadn't, we have agreed to be involved in something we really didn't want to do. Aside from there being several possibly healthy reasons why we do agree, there leaves the other larger percentage of time, when we really should have said no.

Four Reasons for Saying YES When We Should Say NO

1. We are fearful of disapproval, of not being liked.

2. We feel the need to take care of others, putting them ahead of ourselves.

3. We want to feel capable.

4. We want to be in control.

Again, it is important to listen carefully to the messages that we impart to ourselves. Are we being supportive and encouraging, affirming that we need to take care of how we conduct our lives and how we think about ourselves? Go ahead and ask yourself these simple questions, when considering how you would like to respond to a request for you to help:

- Do I really desire to do this?

- Do I have the time to do this?

- Will this contribute to my overall well-being?

- What are my reasons for wanting to say "yes"?

How you answer these questions is of great importance. You have to be honest and not fall into old patterns of thinking. Instead, you need to be clearing out the clutter of an overly busy life, and this is one way to begin. If your answer to the first three questions is "no," then it is imperative that you have a highly compelling answer for the fourth question, to warrant a "yes" to the request. It is essential to establish clear boundaries. We can achieve this by making certain we give very clear responses. When we say "maybe," we are opening ourselves up to complexity and stress of having to still deal with the situation sometime in the future. When we say "no" and mean it, we are taking good care of ourselves and are being respectful within the relationship with the person making the request. They will come to respect that we are direct and not interested in muddied communications and ambiguous intentions.

How Can You Say No and Feel More Comfortable?

1. Be clear on your values and know what is important to you.

2. Write down your personal desires and goals and prepare time to accomplish them. When you visibly see your plans in writing, this will assist you in saying "no."

3. If you prefer to communicate in difficult situations by email or phone, feel free to do so. It will help you to accomplish your goal of saying "no" more easily.

4. Be firm in your communication of "no." You do not need to justify or explain your reasons for declining. Be polite, clear, and concise.

Learning to say "no" will offer you a great satisfaction in the planning of your life. Your time will become your own and you will feel liberated from feeling beholden to do something you really do not want to do. It is very empowering to say this very small and simple word. When you practice doing this on a regular basis and become comfortable with the process, you will feel a sense of confidence and autonomy that you are in charge of the choices you make.

Learning to say "no" will offer you a great satisfaction in the planning of your life.

Relationships

Clearly we care very deeply for the people we love and it is a pleasure to be able to do nice things for them. However, it is important to examine the nature of how we function, overall, within our families, with our friends, within in our businesses and generally, out in the world. We must ask ourselves the following questions:

1. Are we equally respectful to ourselves as we are with others?

2. Do we carefully choose our words when communicating and interacting in all of our relationships?

3. Have we actively chosen to have all these people in our lives, or have some of them just found their way in and don't really serve a positive purpose for being there at all?

Some people have a way of lifting us up while others have a terrible talent of bringing us down. It is vitally important to value ourselves. One way we can accomplish this is by being highly selective about whom we actually spend our time with, as we only have so much! It is important to understand that it is completely appropriate to choose to end certain relationships when they do not contribute to our overall well-being. Sometimes though, many of us have a difficult time doing this because it goes against how we were raised and what we were taught.

Robert and Samantha had been dating for just over a year, and in the beginning, Samantha had told Robert how kind and thoughtful he was. Robert was sweet, often bringing her flowers, but after a few months, Samantha was becoming pouty and remote. Flowers were no longer enough to satisfy her. She wanted jewelry and constant attention and didn't want Robert to spend time with his own friends. Robert tried to accommodate Samantha's wishes, but he was becoming increasingly unhappy as the months passed. Robert told her he wanted to spend time not only with her, but with his friends, as well, but she became even more insistent that he decide to spend his free time exclusively with her or that their relationship was over. After carefully thinking about the last year he had spent with Samantha, he realized how unhappy he had become. Robert wanted to see his friends and he didn't want to feel unhappy and powerless any longer. He wanted to feel like himself again and knew the only way to accomplish that was to end his toxic relationship. Though Samantha tried to manipulate and cajole, Robert stood firmly with how he felt, and he successfully ended the relationship.

....

It is vitally important to value ourselves.

....

Despite the fact that this idea may make us uncomfortable, we need to learn to be able to do this and clear out the clutter within our relationships. It is a highly valuable exercise to take a careful look at the significant relationships we have and determine how we actually feel about each one of them. A good place to start is with our family and our friends, by asking ourselves the following questions:

- Are they supportive of me?

- Do they actively listen to me?

- How do they help me to accomplish my goals?

We are born into our families, and far too often there is an unrealistic standard of expectation that says we must love and encourage one another, *no matter what*. But is this really healthy? Is this a good practice? Perhaps you have a brother who was selfish and never very kind to you, or parents who were glaringly absent while you were growing up, but now they are demanding your attention, your care, your help. Is it appropriate to give them your positive energy just because they want it *now*? Why is it that we feel we have to continue on being dedicated at all costs, as if we were still the child who had Leaped into those early relationships? Wouldn't you think that kindness and respect should factor in somewhere?

In our efforts to honestly answer these questions, we may come to realize that our sister is jealous of us and really has little interest in supporting our desires. Or perhaps it is our dad, who had never traveled the world as he had hoped and now can only find fault with our desire to backpack through South America. Whatever answers we may come up with, we need to be willing to take an honest look and be strong enough to take appropriate action. Is it right that we should allow ourselves to be bombarded by unkind words and undermining thoughts from others? Or wouldn't it be far better to discover a way to respect ourselves and do what is right?

Solutions

Creating clear boundaries within our relationships is very important to do. If after asking ourselves our three questions: Are they supportive of me? Do they actively listen to me? and How do they help me to accomplish my goals?, we discover that the person in question does not truly have our best interests at heart, then it is likely time to alter the nature of how we interact with them. If after making it clear that you are no longer willing to have them relate to you in an undesirable way, you could instead remove yourself and stay physically at a distance from them.

....

Creating clear boundaries within our relationships is very important to do.

....

Eva's mother had always loved her, but was often overbearing in how she related to her daughter. From the time that Eva was a little girl, her mom told her what she should wear and who her friends should be. She constantly corrected her on her behavior and manners, leaving little time for Eva to just be a child. Throughout the years, Eva listened well and tried to accommodate her mother's wishes, but when Eva had her first serious boyfriend in high school, her mother didn't think he was good enough for her daughter, while in fact, he was really quite wonderful. Her mom told her she could no longer see him, but that didn't work. Then she began to remove privileges and that only strained their relationship further. Despite the strain and discomfort with her mom, Eva continued to see her boyfriend during after-school activities and events. And after her senior year had ended and Eva went off to college, she happily continued to see her boyfriend, but didn't go home to see her mother as frequently as she might have.

It is not a life requirement to allow yourself to be treated in any way that makes you feel less than whole and incapable of making good decisions, even though within your family, it may have been an implicit rule. The point is, we can choose differently. We can choose to unclutter our lives, by distancing ourselves from these negative relationships that are not supportive and positive. Instead of continuing to be in close proximity with these negative influences, we could choose to love them from afar. There are numerous ways in which we can accomplish this. Here are a few ideas:

- Minimize phone calls and emails.

- Attend family gatherings where the negative behaviors occur only as absolutely necessary.

- Keep your personal business to yourself; don't offer up ammunition.

- Create clear, positive boundaries in how you allow them to behave with you.

Yes, our families will always be our families and likely the most difficult people to make changes with. However, we do have relationships with others outside of our families, and unless we are actively enjoying being with those people, there is no requirement that we have to keep them in our lives. It is your privilege to choose whom you want to spend your time with. Be bold enough to clear out the clutter, if these relationships are not desirable and supportive of the person you want to be.

Obviously, it is easy to walk away from an acquaintance, but not so easy to walk away from an employer. If you are feeling compromised while at your job, remember: There are things you can do to improve your situation. We can try the following:

- We can stay in the job and do our best to emotionally distance ourselves from the person.

- We can discuss our concerns with the person and establish clear boundaries with how we want to be treated.

- We can focus on enjoying the work we are doing while minimizing our attention directed at the other person.

- We can decide to clear out the clutter and let the job go.

There are variations on the process and the outcome, but it is for us to choose how we want to proceed. The power is in making our own decisions and then implementing what we choose.

We all experience a wide range of differing relationships in all that we do. Whether we find ourselves at work, at school, at home, or simply out shopping, we are in a relationship with every other person we meet. It is essentially important to surround ourselves with interesting and positive people so that we may create an atmosphere of warmth and encouragement, as we begin to craft a life we desire to live. We need to remember to clear out the clutter when someone is not a healthy person to be with. We need to know it is okay to let them go. When we are in healthy relationships with people who are living lives that are actively inspired, we too will benefit from what they are doing, just as we will create a positive effect on how they feel within themselves.

15.

Tending to Mind, Body, and Spirit

AFFIRMATION

I am my body, my mind, and my spiritual self. When I create, I am connecting that which I am in my essential nature with who I am as a human being. My creative expression is a reflection of all that I am. I will trust my intuitive guidance that leads me to know what is highest and best for me.

It is a very bad idea to defer joy. When we defer joy, we risk our health, our happiness, our productivity, and the relationships we share with those whom we cherish most. When we blindly chug along down those narrow tracks toward that Grand Destination of *later*, we squander our potential to experience a life directed by joy and creativity, both now and along our way. It is important for us to take the steps to discover that which we truly love to do, embracing each moment in that doing as the precious destination it actually is. We must come to understand that it is not the Grand Destinations dangling in our idea of *later* that bring us the greatest joy. Instead, it is for us to become utterly awakened to the fact that it is the simple things we embrace each day that truly will make our hearts sing.

> *When we defer joy, we risk our health, our happiness, our*
> *productivity, and the relationships we share with those*
> *whom we cherish most.*

We all have any army of reasons why we can't write that novel, train for a marathon, or study the night sky's sparkling constellations. We think we are too busy, too tired, and over-committed. We have people to take care of, jobs to do, errands to tend to, and so when we arrive home from a long and challenging day, we just want to relax. What do we collectively do? We turn on the television and choose to tune out. So if we are constantly running all day and grab the TV remote at night, how are we going to create the time that we think we don't have? How are we possibly going to come to the awareness that it is essential to do what we love every single day of our life?

When we come to understand that we need to tenderly care for all aspects of our being, we will have begun the process of moving ourselves into balance, blending together the needs of our minds, our bodies, and our spiritual essence. Because many of us have ignored directly caring for ourselves for far too long, we wonder how we are going to change our patterns and begin anew. What is it that we need to focus on?

There are lots of things that we can do, but a simple way to start is by keeping our physical selves healthy and our minds actively inspired; we need to create a sense of peace in all that we do, even when we are vitally active. When we begin to think about how we truly want to live our lives, we must be willing to open to the harmonious energy that our creative inspirations will require, to be born into a physical reality. It is when we combine our creative potential with our dynamically inspired desire that we will create an outward expression that reflects our internal beauty.

When we learn to consistently think good thoughts and focus on our bodies being healthy and well, this is a good beginning on our pathway to wholeness and happiness. It is imperative that we know that we are worthy to be loved by another and actively want to love in return. This allows us to open to the Streaming joy that we want flowing in and out of our hearts. We need to develop our ability to sit quietly in our place of peace and call in the wisdom of our spiritual Essence, which offers us the gifts of solitude and renewal. And when these pieces are all present and singing in concert with one another, we will have become a beautiful symphony in body, mind, and spirit: the happy and attuned person we were born to be.

How are we possibly going to come to the awareness that it is essential to do what we love every single day of our life?

Avoidance

Why, might we ask, do we avoid doing things that we love to do? Of course, there are a number of reasons this can happen. Perhaps we no longer know what we truly enjoy because we are too busy taking care of everyone else, or maybe we went down a different path than what we had loved when we were little and don't feel as though there is any turning back. But it is extremely painful for us to *not do* the things that create meaning and value for us. Perhaps this is the most compelling, causative agent behind human pain, as it fabricates a gash within the fabric of our being, so that we are no longer able to experience ourselves as one unified whole. When we don't do what we are Called to do, we become compromised within our emotions, within our minds, and within in our bodies. Illness has a way of creeping into abandoned hearts and causing great afflictions of the body and spirit.

If we truly want to live as a beautiful and radiant version of who we Leaped in here to be, then we must take the time to discover what we love to do and find a way to do it. The silent truth is this: It is agonizing for the human spirit to live a life of mediocrity and repetition, when our hearts surely know how it is supposed to be.

Taking Care of Our Mind, Our Body, and Our Spirit

As we discussed, clutter is a detriment to every aspect of our lives and it is essential that we successfully clear out the clutter within our minds. When we are not able to do this, we have the tendency to tire more quickly and we can't seem to focus on our own thoughts. Of course, there are simple things that we can do to soothe our wearied minds such as relaxing or sleeping, but one of the most effective things we can do to help ourselves is to learn to meditate. Let's begin by looking more carefully at what meditation actually is and how it can have a positive effect on us.

Meditation is a practice designed to create an awareness of the present moment through the use of concentrated focus, breath, sound, or attention on an object, most often resulting in a state of relaxation and calm. It is a wonderful way to bring us back to center, almost like having a reset button built into us. By starting and ending our day with meditation, it would greatly benefit us in every aspect of our beings. Meditation can be as simple as sitting quietly and concentrating on a lighted candle or focusing on one thought. Rhythmic breathing is also helpful for quieting our body and calming our mind, and by putting all these ingredients together into one practice, they can create a very effective result for us.

PRACTICE—Simple Meditation for Calming the Mind

Find a comfortable and safe place to sit or lie down. You may set the tone by lighting candles and making sure your body will not become chilled or overheated.

Begin by taking in a deep breath, inhaling a calming energy, and drawing it into your body through the top of your head, down through your spine, and expanding into all parts of your body. Feel this beautiful energy filling you up, and as you exhale, allow it to release all the collected energies of stress and strain, to be carried out through your arms and your legs, reaching your hands and your feet, and then releasing the energy in entirety. Again, breathe in deeply, imagining that you are drawing up the energy of the Earth through the soles of your feet, welcoming love and warmth to calm your being. Exhale deeply. And when you take in your third breath, breathe in the beauty of your conscious Essence and combine that with the grounding of your physical world, drawing in from both your head and your feet.

As you begin to feel the currents of happiness flowing into you, you are feeling relaxed, welcoming in a gentle peace. Continue your slow, easy breathing, and begin to think about creating your days to be happy and joyful. Allow yourself to consider what that might look like for you. Imagine feeling good in all that you do, whether you are at work or play. Welcome in the feeling of ease as you take care of your responsibilities, while you tenderly nurture the beautiful person that you are. Take time now to let yourself drift. Embrace your feelings and invite them in to become your own.

Let us breathe in deeply, drawing in the grounding energy of our beautiful Earth again. Feel its strength flowing through your veins, into your heart, into all parts of your body. Exhale gently and slowly. Now breathe in again, welcoming the current of consciousness to enter through the top of your head and let it radiate out into your body, out into your hands and into your feet. Breathe in a third time, welcoming the connection of our Essence and Form, and feel gratitude for the inspired gift of creation that resides within you.

Know that as you open your eyes, you are feeling the fresh beginnings of creating a life you love, by taking charge of creating how your day unfolds. Try to do your Practice three times each day, welcoming in the active energy of the morning, moving through the afternoon, and then embracing the peace that is born from having experienced a day well-lived. With your eyes now fully opened, feel the joy of being inspired and productive. Welcome the peace of a calm mind and embrace the gift of nurturing wonderful you.

Body

It is important to have a healthy body and we need to do all we can to positively impact our physical well-being. When we are physically well, then we are able to carry out all the other activities within our lives in a far more enjoyable way. In the case of physical health, routines are advantageous to keeping our body working as it should. By taking responsibility for creating a healthy body, we are in turn contributing to enjoying a healthy spirit within.

....

By taking responsibility for creating a healthy body, we are in turn contributing to enjoying a healthy spirit within.

....

Here are a few simple steps that will allow us to stay healthy and fit, supporting us to be well in mind, body, and spirit.

- Enjoy your evenings as a time to rest. After a busy day, we need downtime to relax and restore our essential selves.

- Deep, peacefully restful sleep every night is a must—on average, eight hours is excellent.

- Limit your tea, coffee, and other stimulating food and drink by day, so that you are able to sleep easily and soundly when you slip into bed at night.

- Be physically active. Find an activity that you really enjoy and do it. Perhaps you might like walking or running, or riding a bicycle might be more to your taste. There are team sports and individual sports, or you can choose to go to a gym. What matters most is that you are staying active as a regular part of your daily and weekly routine.

- Eat fresh foods, including raw vegetables and fruit every day.

- Drink an abundance of clean water.

- Avoid overeating and abandon unhealthy habits. If you have negative habits, focus on quitting smoking and taking unprescribed drugs, and stop overindulging in alcohol. Create a plan to terminate anything that does not soulfully feed you.

- Stretching or a gentle yoga is a wonderful way to remain flexible and to be calm.

- As with all things, moderation is optimal.

Spirit

Maintaining a healthy spiritual balance requires conscious effort on our part. When we nurture our creative spirit within, we are connecting with our essential source of wisdom. In order for us to align ourselves with the Essence of who we are, we must bring our lives into balance in every possible way. Far too often we neglect our precious bodies and our beautiful minds, forgetting that we are so much more than these little human beings who Leaped into these lives with a very specific mission of our own.

....

When we nurture our creative spirit within, we are connecting with our essential source of wisdom.

....

When we are finally able to understand that we are truly the physical expression of that which we are in Essence, we will develop the capacity to embrace our own unique Genius. When this transformation occurs, we will move into a beautiful alignment of body, mind, and spirit as we become a joyful expression in our wholeness of being.

We also must be reminded that we are an integral component in our family of humankind. Just as we must create balance within our individual spiritual selves, so we must open to living as part of the collective whole. We are not meant to live in an isolated manner. Isolation is not remotely synonymous with solitude. Isolation is an aberration of the spiritual expression, serving only to knock us out of balance. It is when we each embrace our own life's purpose and share it out in the world that my purpose can commune with your purpose, and together we will create a uniquely beautiful work of art.

As we can see, it is essentially important to surround ourselves by inspired people, so that we may flourish within the spirit of supportive, healthy relationships. The following practice is designed to help us find the people whom we are meant to be with: open-minded, heart-warming friends who want to make the world a better place by living a meaningful life designed for them.

PRACTICE—Surrounding Ourselves with Positive People

Positive, supportive people are not difficult to spot. They are happy and interesting and usually have a great attitude about most everything they do. Though they are likely very busy, they will always stop to offer encouragement and support to those who are making an effort to do something good with their lives. These are the people who have figured out what they want to be doing and are actively engaged in doing it. They are the same people we would like to have in our lives as we turn our attention to balancing ourselves in body, mind, and spirit and creating a life of meaning and purpose.

EXERCISE 1

List five qualities that define a positive and inspired person:

1. _____

2. _____

3. _____

4. _____

5. _____

If you want your list to be longer, feel free to add as many qualities that seem valuable to you. Take a bit of time and truly think about what is most important to you.

EXERCISE 2

List five qualities about yourself that you most respect:

1. _____

2. _____

3. _____

4. _____

5. _____

When you have taken your time and completed your lists, carefully look at both of them. Do you see any similarities? Do you have some of the same qualities that you used to describe a positive and inspired person? How wonderful, if you do, but if there is something in the first list that you consider valuable and would also like to embrace within yourself, take the time to think about it and decide that you want to bring that into your life.

Once you have decided what is most important to you, you can create an affirmation that you can use throughout your day. For example:

AFFIRMATION:

I am committed to creating _____ within my life.

(for example, Focus)

Whatever the quality may be, you can fill in the blank and apply it to this affirmation. If you desire to become more focused, the affirmation could be expanded and spoken aloud or written out in this way:

AFFIRMATION:

I am a focused human being. I set my attention on
that which is essentially important to me and follow
through until I am done. I am committed to giving

myself the gift of focus, allowing me to experience
the joy of single-mindedly working within my cre-
ative process.

Yes, we have the ability to create a beautiful and healthy life, by focusing on caring for ourselves. When all of the components of who we are are primed and flowing smoothly, the essence of our remarkable spirit will guide us in living a balanced and inspired life.

16.

Creating Time to Be Alone

AFFIRMATION

*I welcome in the beauty of quiet, allowing myself to be calm and
at ease. I value the gift of solitude as I allow my creative self to
retreat from the busy-ness of living, into my own personal space
of peace and grace.*

Do you ever just sit down in a quiet place and allow yourself to
simply *Be*, without looking at a magazine or listening to music,
without watching television or reading a book? Do you ever just
find a calm place and invite yourself to not think a conscious
thought, but rather, allow yourself to drift and relax into not
doing anything at all? The truth is, this is a very important thing
to do, yet somehow we don't seem to give ourselves this kind of
downtime. Taking time for ourselves is often viewed as selfish by
those who want our constant attention, but as we awaken to our
creative Essence and begin to live a life that Calls to us, we will
soon discover that creating solitude is a life-saving act.

Solitude is the state of being alone and away from others,
without feeling any sense of regret, guilt, or loneliness. Spending
time in solitude is highly self-nurturing and a practice that we all
need to embrace. When we are so busy with the hectic activities
of our lives and constantly giving our time away to others, we
become depleted and worn down when we don't take the time

to fill ourselves back up. Running on empty can only last for so long. Just as we need to refuel our vehicles that get us from here to there, so we must also refuel ourselves in mind, body, and spirit, so that we may be happy, productive, and healthy. Yes, we want to be generous and kind in our caring for those we love, but as we were reminded earlier on, we must be sure to put our own oxygen mask on first, before we can possibly help anyone else around us.

Spending time in solitude is highly self-nurturing and a practice that we all need to embrace.

We need to learn to value ourselves and not slip into a misguided mindset that it is a virtuous thing to be present for everyone else while abandoning our own needs. When we discover that what we want to do conflicts with the desires of those we care for, and we continually defer to their wants and needs, eventually we will become duly frustrated and angry inside. Over time, if we continue to put ourselves last, we are going to experience an emotional concussion or suffer a slow, tedious death of spirit, by perpetually living a life of compromise and mediocrity. We must become aware that if we continue to function in this way, we are putting ourselves at risk of losing our essential individuality to the wants and needs of others, and this is a very unwise and debilitating thing to do.

Solitude is an essential ingredient within every human being's life. Yet how many of us are really comfortable being alone, without distractions and activities that keep us engaged and busy? We need time to be by ourselves, so that we may relax, reflect, and create a sense of peace within. We need time alone so that we can examine our lives, to see what must go and what we want to stay. It is important to clear out the clutter that is taking up space in our lives and begin to thoughtfully introduce doing things that we truly love to do. Taking the time to think on these things is a very important step, and we must be very careful not to allow anyone or anything to get in its way.

When We Begin to Change

When we begin to make changes in our lives, it is a common occurrence for those around us to not be supportive and encouraging of what we are doing. They may feel threatened that we are changing, feeling as though we are leaving them behind and excluding them from being front and center in our lives. We may find that some will try to sabotage what we are doing or try to entice us away from our new personal mission. All the same, it is essential to take the time and space for this private, internal reflection, even when we don't feel that we know what we are doing. It is when we begin something new and focus our energy and intention on that action, while disallowing others to pull us off-track, that we will experience an unseen force that seems to help us on our way. Perhaps it is our Guide who has our back, encouraging us to stay on our path, and as Ralph Waldo Emerson insightfully said, "To be yourself in a world that is constantly trying to make you something else, is the greatest accomplishment." The bottom line is, we have to just do it.

Creating Quiet

We need to give ourselves the quiet that we require. As creative people, which we all are in our own way, we need time to relax and be at ease, allowing ourselves to become refreshed and renewed. It is important for us to release our tension, anger, and resentments that we harbor deeply within ourselves. It is highly possible that many of us may be unaware that we are harboring these kinds of feelings at all, but as we begin to create the time for solitude within our lives, we are likely to run up against burdensome feelings we weren't overtly aware of. It is important to know that this is a natural progression and to be expected. Creating quiet is a wonderful opportunity for us, so that we may retreat into ourselves and become refreshed and renewed. It may also be a time for healing old wounds and upsets in a safe and comforting way. This is a place where we will come to realize that we are not alone and lonely, especially when we are all by ourselves. This is the place where we can begin to become our own adoring friend and take care of the special person that we actually are.

The art of living our lives is the most expansive and creative endeavor we will ever undertake, quite simply because living our lives encompasses every thought that has graced our mind, every word uttered from our mouths, every tear that has burned our cheeks, and every kiss or hug we have ever yearned for. Living our lives is the ultimate act in our artistically creative endeavors, embracing everything we will ever think, do, or be. Let's turn our attention to initiating ways to effectively create the quiet and solitude we all need so badly, so that we can heighten our ability to enjoy all we do, every single day.

Let's turn our attention to initiating ways to effectively create the quiet and solitude we all need so badly, so that we can heighten our ability to enjoy all we do, every single day.

Of course, we have experienced how a stimulating flow of incoming information can be inspiring and exciting, but as with all things, we need to create a balance with just how much exposure we allow ourselves to the hustle and bustle of the world each day. When we take in too much information for an extended period of time, this high level of activity can cause our brains to go on overload, subsequently repressing our creative responses. We need to unplug from our computers, televisions, cell phones, and all the activities we have loaded into our lives, giving ourselves the opportunity to calm down so that we may awaken other pathways of our creative expression to be able to flow into us.

Now, let's consider some of the ways in which we can comfortably create this solitude and quiet that we justly merit.

PRACTICE—Creating Quiet and Stillness— the Art of Not-Doing

• Being out in nature is one of the most restorative things you can do. Whether you live close to woods or a body of water, or even in a city, find a place where you can sit alone, freely without interruption. Feel the calming effects of sitting under a tree, on a beach, or on a park bench. Relax into being in nature, wherever you may find it. Allow all your thoughts to slowly drift away.

• Create your own private place within your home where you can relax and sit quietly without interruption. A corner of your room or closet will do nicely. Having a comfortable place where you can sit or lie down is important. Close the door to your outside world and enjoy doing absolutely nothing at all. If you are having trouble letting yourself go, take a few slow, deep breaths and release— everything! This is your time.

• Meditation is a nice way to create the calm you need. Take five minutes to meditate, bringing yourself to a calm, quiet place inside you. After you have finished your meditation, open your eyes and simply let yourself remain in the calm and relaxed state you just created.

• Journaling is an effective way to release the busy thoughts racing through our minds. Sit down with a notebook that you use expressly for this purpose. Take pencil or pen in hand and let your thoughts flow out onto the paper. Write until you feel yourself become quiet. Close the book and welcome the simplicity of peace that follows.

MEDITATION—Preparing Yourself to Welcome In the Quiet

- Sit or lie down in a quiet, comfortable place.

- Let your body begin to relax as you inhale a lovely, deep breath. Feel the oxygen fill your lungs and release the breath, allowing the tension in your shoulders to let go with the outbreath.

- Breathe in again, sensing the tension in your chest loosen, and when you exhale, release that tightness, feeling it exiting through your hands and feet.

- Inhale a third time, welcoming clear energy to come in through the top of your head.

- As you are exhaling, feel the activity in your brain begin to slow down as you allow your thoughts to gently slip away.

- Continue your breathing, focusing on releasing the activity within your mind, allowing your breath to clear out its pathways, sweeping away all thought.

- Soften your breathing and feel the peace. While remaining in this relaxed state, open your eyes and allow yourself to simply *Be*.

The Benefits of Creating Solitude

When we take the time to experience solitude, we will give ourselves the gift of peace within and the possibility to experience a wondrous, creative Streaming in all our actions. Here is a list of some of the benefits that creating solitude provides us:

- We will have the capacity to enjoy our relationships with others more, as a result of giving ourselves this self-nurturing time to become calm and centered.

- After a period of quiet, wonderful ideas tend to filter into our consciousness. As we are more open and receptive, infused with a feeling of inspired joy, we allow our imaginations to flow freely.

- We become healthier in mind, body, and spirit, feeling less deprived of time and more buoyant with joy.

- When we embrace quiet, it often leads us to welcome in time for fun and play, as a counterpoint and balance.

- We garner fresh insights into previously challenging problems.

- We will increase our awareness of the world around us.

- We will be calm, and when we are calm, we are able to eliminate nervous, frenetic energy.

PRACTICE—Solitude in Motion: The Art of Quietly Doing by Yourself

The next step in creating solitude for ourselves is bringing the quiet into gentle action. Here are some ways to enjoy your experience of solitude, as you put it into gentle motion:

- Spend time in your garden.

- Practice yoga as a meditation.

- Take a beautiful walk out into nature—walking is a moving meditation, a way of creating peace in motion.

- Read quietly by a warm fire or outside in a hammock.

- Enjoy your coffee or tea in the morning, reading or simply gazing out the window.

- Wander through a bookstore or some other place that interests you—no need to purchase—window shopping can be pleasurable, too.

- Take a long, hot bath or shower.

- Listen to music, play an instrument, paint or draw.

- Dance, knit, sculpt, build with your hands.

- Sail, walk, go to an art museum.

Feel free to add to this list. Write down some of your own ideas.

Creating the Time for Solitude

It is vitally important to create time for quiet and solitude, though it is an area in our lives that we often fail to prioritize. In the next chapter, there will be exercises for creating the time we don't think we have, so that we may begin doing things that are not only enjoyable and enriching, but also healthy for us in all aspects of Being. As we begin to create the time for quiet and solitude, we will become more present in the moment and able to focus on what really matters most. We will learn to listen to the whispers within us, guiding us to be bold and daring enough to release the restraint of the architectural framework that has held us captive for far too long.

17.

Doing What You Love

AFFIRMATION

I am committed to living a life that I truly love and doing things that I enjoy, every single day. I believe in me and will give myself time for solitude and reflection, and time to immerse myself in activities that fulfill my creative spirit.

When we were children, most of us knew what we loved to do. We were passionate about so many things and let our imaginations run freely. But for some of us, as the responsibilities and pressures of life developed, we became immersed in tending to what we thought we needed to do. We became busier by the day, and as the years passed, we discovered that we no longer remembered what it was we had once been passionate about. We found ourselves caught in a fast-paced life that didn't allow for us to travel the world, to write that book, or play a round of golf each week.

Perhaps, though, your story is a little bit different. Maybe you do remember what it was that you loved as a child and know very well what it is that you enjoy now, but simply don't feel you have the time or the ability to do it. Either way, what is most important is for us to learn how to create the time that we don't think we have and then create a plan to be able to actually make wonderful use of it. As we just learned, spending time alone and creating a sense of peace within is essential to encouraging our creative spirit to open up and tap into our natural inclinations. It is from within this place of simplicity that we can safely allow ourselves to think about what we would like to be doing, and then create a plan to actually get started.

It is from within this place of simplicity that we can safely allow ourselves to think about what we would like to be doing, and then create a plan to actually get started.

PRACTICE—Identifying What You Liked to Do from Childhood

Make a list of what you enjoyed doing when you were young. If you are experiencing any resistance to doing this, try taking a few slow, deep breaths and let your mind begin to wander. Allow your imagination to flow freely. Perhaps it might help if you begin from a more recent year and then subsequently move backward in time. How early on you can remember?

At twenty years old, I loved to _____

At fifteen years old, I loved to _____

At ten years old, I loved to _____

At five years old, I loved to _____

At three years old, I loved to _____

At _____ years old, I loved to _____

After you have taken a journey through the years and have written down what you enjoyed doing at each approximate age, review what you have written and see if you can find any repeating patterns. For example, you might discover that some of your responses look similar to these:

- At five years old, I loved to sing and dance.

- At ten years old, I loved learning how to play the piano and taking ballet.

- At fifteen years old, I loved being in a rock band and was the lead singer and dancer.

- At twenty years old, I loved moving to New York City and auditioning on Broadway.

Obviously, there is a very clear pattern that developed here, where music and dance were driving forces throughout this person's life. But often, making this kind of connection from childhood isn't quite that easy. Sometimes we have to be patient and be willing to dig a little deeper.

In contrast to this example where music, dance, and performance were driving this person forward, you might also find that you have written down a series of seemingly unrelated interests that you enjoyed throughout your years while growing up. As I described earlier on, this was more the nature of my experience. I loved to play piano, to write, to speak, and to watch things grow. My interests fanned out into many different directions, but fascinatingly enough, most of the very same interests I had when I was a child continue to play a significant role in my current life as an adult.

PRACTICE—Identifying What You Like to Do from Adulthood

Now, let's do something similar, but this time, we will fill out our list from the perspective of being ourselves, as the adults we are now. Do your best to relax into this practice, allowing yourself to have fun. Write down what spontaneously comes to you, and then take some time to expand your list further, if you would like.

List as many things as you can think of, in no particular order of importance.

Here is an example:

AS AN ADULT, I enjoy working outside in my garden.

Now you try it:

As an adult, I enjoy _____
_____.

As an adult, I enjoy _____
_____.

As an adult, I enjoy _____
_____.

As an adult, I enjoy _____
_____.

As an adult, I enjoy _____
_____.

Now that you have taken some time for careful consideration and have completed your list, take a few minutes to read it aloud to yourself. Perhaps you wrote down that you enjoy playing golf, going to yoga classes, or that you love to go out onto the slopes and ski. Or maybe you expressed your enjoyment of sewing, traveling, or studying French. Of course, the possibilities are endless! What is it that you have on your list? Take your time and allow yourself to relax into imagining what it is that you would like to do. After you have finished, review your responses. Do you see any patterns emerging? Are you currently doing any of the things in your life now that you just wrote down?

Some of us may have a very long list, while others of us may not have been able to think of even one thing we want to do. Sometimes life has a way of blocking those thoughts from us, but if we look back into the list from our childhood, it might just offer us a clue. That is the whole point. Very often, the things that we loved when we were small are the very same things that we love now, even though we may not be consciously aware of it.

Very often, the things that we loved when we were small are the very same things that we love now, even though we may not be consciously aware of it.

Now, once again, sit quietly and carefully look at your two lists, side-by-side. Is there one idea that seems more interesting than any other on there? It really doesn't matter which list it comes from; just choose one thing you think you might like to try more than any other. Once you have made your selection, put your lists aside and do the following practice.

PRACTICE—Focusing on Doing the One Thing You Just Chose to Do

- Close your eyes and sit quietly. Breathe in and exhale several times, quieting your body and mind.

- Let your awareness of your physical surroundings slip away and simply focus on the one thing you have just chosen to do.

- Begin to focus on the idea you are interested in. For example, if you just decided that you want to climb a mountain, think about what it is that appeals to you about this idea. Perhaps you like the thought of standing on the very peak of the mountaintop to feel the power and majesty of that experience.

- What is it that draws you to want to do this thing?

- Let yourself drift into a place of wondering. With our example of climbing a mountain, could it be the idea of the physical challenge, of getting strong and fit enough to actually be able to accomplish this goal, that calls out to you?

- Apply this to your activity. Continue with this line of imagining. Maybe it is as simple as liking the idea of wearing hiking boots and carrying the gear you might need, or simply being out in the fresh air, feeling on top of the world.

- Understand that there are many uncomplicated reasons that generate a desire within us, and it is best to try to focus in on that good feeling we experienced when we dreamed up our idea in the first place.

- Once you have settled on what it is that appeals to you, allow yourself to let your thoughts roam freely, without limitation. Feel the joy and the power of the moment. Feel the cool breeze of the mountain air; welcome the solitude and beauty of nature. Immerse yourself as much as possible in the experience you are creating, for as long as you desire.

- Now, begin consciously breathing again, bringing yourself back to your present awareness of where you are sitting, being sure to hold on to that pleasant feeling you were just enjoying.

So, if it was painting that you focused on, were you able to connect with the artist in you, who once loved to color and now wants to paint? Did you imagine yourself as the athlete you always wanted to be, and now you are going to learn to play tennis? Whatever it is that excites you enough to want to try it, that is the feeling you need to focus on manifesting when you begin to actually create a way to do what you desire.

Of course, it is best to start with something simple, so that you will have the ability to schedule it into your life on a regular basis. While you may not be able to afford the time or the expense of traveling to Italy to sketch the Sistine Chapel, you can certainly go to the library or on the Internet and find remarkable photos to stand in as your model. All you would need are the most basic supplies and a little time to get started.

Understand, you may not get a clear answer from simply trying this one time. If you were not able to get a satisfying response, allow a day or two to pass and repeat the exercise once again. Do not give up. Within a few tries, you will get results, and once you do, you will be ready to begin. You will be prepared to do something that you love for fifteen minutes every day.

18.

Fifteen Minutes a Day—Creating Time We Don't Think We Have

There are two highly effective practices that can help us to alter the patterns of our lives, so that we can begin to move into designing our own futures. Neither practice is difficult to actually do; we simply need to make them become our priority and then focus on following through.

The first practice is doing something that we enjoy for fifteen minutes every day, *no matter what*. The second practice we need to master is learning how to create the time that we don't think we have, so that we can generate a place of calm and quiet within ourselves while doing what it is we want to do. With a little focus and effort, we will learn how to do both of these things, and eventually, do them very well. What is most important in both of these practices, in fact in all the practices within this book, is that we must learn how to make a commitment and then follow through. It really is that simple.

Fifteen Minutes a Day to Do What You Love

Imagine how you might feel if, upon awakening each morning, you knew you were going to do something you truly enjoyed, and then from every day forward, you would continue with this plan.

Over time, imagine how this might begin to create a shift in you, making you feel more positive and bright. Don't you think it just might be possible that after creating a wonderful new habit of taking care of yourself in this way, those fifteen minutes might very likely expand into thirty minutes, then an hour, and maybe even more? There is much to be said about beginning anything new. When we make the effort to begin, this intention sets into motion a new energy that previously did not exist. By focusing and implementing our plan for fifteen minutes a day, this seemingly simple action will allow us to break through the restrictions and inertia that have kept us locked into an old pattern of living, allowing us to shift into a beautiful new pathway of our very own design.

Let us begin.

PRACTICE—Fifteen Minutes a Day

- Carefully review the lists that you created, of what you would like to do, both from when you were a child and as an adult. Do you see any similarities between the two? What are they? Write them down.

- Do you observe any differences? What are they? Write them down.

- Is there one thing on either of those two lists that really jumps out at you, calling for you to do it now?

Choose one thing from either of your lists that you can integrate within your day. This means that you can readily do it; it is easy for you and doesn't cost money that you can't afford. Make it be something that you know you can accomplish. Do not worry if you don't think you have the time to do it. We'll take care of that next.

Take a fresh notebook and write on the first page what it is you want to do. For example:

I want to learn how to knit.

I want to grow roses in my garden.

I want to learn to play a musical instrument.

I want to learn about astronomy and study the night sky.

I want to _____
(fill in the blank)

- You get the idea. Now write the date next to what you wrote you would like to do.

- The next step is to select an activity from your list and prepare to actually do it. For example, if you feel like gardening, why not choose that?

- Now, begin. Before you start, write down the time. Do the activity, and when you are finished, again record the time you finished. Also include a brief description of what you did and, very importantly, how it made you feel.

- That's it.

- Put the book away and don't take it out until the next day. If you can do your practice at the same time each day, that is great. It allows for you to create a stronger connection with this process, and that is a valuable thing to do. If your scheduled responsibilities do not allow for you to do this at the same time each day, do not worry. Just do the best that you can.

- As you practice your Fifteen Minutes a Day, repeat the same sequence each time: Document the activity you are doing, the times you started and finished, and how it made you feel.

- Commit to doing this for one month, no excuses. At the end of the month, read through your entries and see how your feelings and thoughts changed over that time period. Do you see any patterns emerging?

- Ask yourself the following questions:

  1. Did I enjoy what I was doing?

  2. In what ways did my thoughts and feelings about this change over the last month?

  3. Did I need to change the activity I started out with?

  4. Did I increase my time each day for what I was doing?

  5. Did I decrease my time?

  6. Did I miss a day, during the month? If so, how did that make me feel?

  7. Do I wish to continue? Do I want to modify what I am doing in any way? If so, what are the changes I would make?

  8. Do I want to change my activity to something new?

  9. Did I hold to my commitment?

  10. Did I receive support from those around me?

  11. Did I experience resistance from them? If yes, how did I address it?

  12. Did I experience resistance within myself? If yes, how did I deal with it?

  13. Other observations?

- At the end of the month, add an entry into your journal, answering the questions above. Feel free to go into detail, remembering that it is all for your own benefit and for your eyes only! Be sure to include the question and then follow it up with your response. Date it. Be honest. Review the content of your answers. Are there any changes that need to be made? Are you ready to sign on for the next thirty days?

- Keep going. You are doing a wonderful job!

Now that you have a month of successful practice under your belt, you will have noticed how quickly fifteen minutes passes, and I would suspect that once you became immersed in what you were doing, you found yourself wanting to go beyond the fifteen-minute commitment. That's okay; in fact, that's great! When we discover that we love what we are doing, it becomes easier to forfeit spending time on things we used to do that really hadn't served us very well in the past.

Creating Time

We have been talking about taking time for quiet each day and for doing things that we enjoy, but how do we find the time within our already busy lives to do this? How do we add in one more activity when we are already over-extended and barely keeping up? How can we possibly begin to create the time that we don't think we have?

The answer is really not as difficult as it may seem; we just need to be willing to try. We need to prioritize. Creating time for solitude is essentially important but we also need to create time for engaging in pleasurable activities that we enjoy, as well. Regardless of what they may be, there are specific things that we can do to be able to make this happen. So where do we begin?

In our fast-paced lives, we are constantly surrounded by a throng of brilliant technology that helps us accomplish fantastic things that weren't available to us even five years ago. Every day, new technologies and applications are rolled out onto the worldwide marketing stage that have been created to streamline all that we do, and of course, they are designed to entertain us in a myriad of ways. We have an infinite selection of premium channels and networks on our televisions, so that we can instantaneously watch almost any film or TV show we could possibly desire. We can read a book or listen to a vast and diverse selection of music on our electronic devices, having the capacity to download them on the spot. We have the luxury to talk with our friends on the other side of the planet, while being able to see one another at the same time. We can conference call and have virtual meetings, drawing participants from all over the globe. It seems that whatever it is that we want, we can almost have it delivered to us immediately. We can connect on Facebook, Instagram, Twitter, LinkedIn, and Google Plus. We can plug into iTunes, YouTube, and online games twenty-four hours a day. But in order to create more time to do the things we really would like to do, we need to stop indulging in the instant gratification of playing with these fascinating technologies that swiftly can become enormously consuming time sponges, if we allow them to.

Creating New Patterns

When we begin to terminate an old pattern of behavior and replace it with a new way of operating, it often feels very challenging, causing us to be inclined to give up too easily. But that is not what we are going to do. No! Instead, we can begin in small ways, taking small bites of time such as in our Fifteen Minutes a Day plan, to teach ourselves new ways of functioning and formatting, so that we may create the desired result we are after.

Suggestions for How to Create Time That We Don't Think We Have

We are all a little bit guilty of thinking that we are so busy and don't have a moment to spare. We think that we are operating at maximum efficiency and top-end speed and that we really don't even have time to consider changing anything. But here are some suggestions that might help you actually modify your thinking about this idea and discover that what is really at play here is that we squander our time in a variety of unconscious ways. The truth is that most of us are highly inefficient with our time management. The very good news is that there are quite a few things that we can do to change this for our own benefit.

The following is a list of suggestions of what we can do, so that we may create the time we don't think we have. Have a look and decide which ones you will try first. I would highly suggest that over time, you try each suggestion and see what offers you the most effective results.

Ten Ways to Create More Time Within Your Daily Life

- When you arrive home at the end of your day, instead of turning on the TV or jumping onto the Internet, you can engage in your desired fifteen-minutes-a-day activity.

- Set your alarm and wake up earlier every day, fifteen minutes to a half hour to start.

- Leave work early; get your business done more quickly and efficiently by focusing and not wasting time during your day.

- Start your workday later; if in school, schedule your classes to start later and give yourself that early-morning time to do as you choose.

- If possible, take a longer lunchtime.

- As you go through your day, refrain from constantly using your mobile device to play games or text. Only do what is necessary. This will create a great deal more time than you might imagine. I know: You like playing on your phone, but this will be worth it in the long run.

- Do not make commitments for after work. Save that time just for you.

- Minimize saying "yes."

- Minimize partying and engaging in unhealthy, sluggish lounging. This only serves to create a state of inertia, which is a self-perpetuating problem.

Assessing and Reviewing Your Options

Once again, take the time to try these ideas and see how they work for you. After a little while, you will know what works best. Choose the methods that give you the more desirable results and stick with them. You can always modify and go back to other ideas, at a later time. After a little practice, you will be creating new patterns and providing yourself with the nurturing that you need. More than likely, you will be enjoying each day more and more as you expand into these suggestions and make them your own personal practice.

Another interesting result I believe you will notice is that as you continue to implement your practices each day, you will find that fifteen minutes just isn't enough time to spend on doing something you enjoy. You will want to be able to dive in more intently, as your interests develop and deepen. Eventually, though, there will come a point when you will feel compelled to go beyond experiencing simple enjoyment. You will find yourself searching for a deeper sense of meaning, to be doing something that feels more valuable to you. A longing will set in, even though you may have no idea what it is that you are actually longing for.

And what could the reason be behind this shift? The practice of doing something that you enjoy for fifteen minutes every day is designed to be a stepping stone upon your path to discovering activities that hold great meaning for you. That is the whole point.

The practice of doing something that you enjoy for fifteen minutes every day is designed to be a stepping stone upon your path to discovering activities that hold great meaning for you.

What's Next?

So, now that you have rearranged your life and have taken a great deal more control over what you are doing, you have given yourself the gift of simplicity, offering you more time to enjoy your solitude and activities that you truly care about. It is a natural progression to feel the need to deepen our experience and discover that which is Calling out to us, becoming aware of what it was we leaped into this life to do. Now, though, it is time to identify our truest talents and abilities—our Genius within— and dynamically Octave our experience of doing something we enjoy into living our life's Calling, with the support and encouragement of our very patient Guide.

19.

Answering the Call

"In the final analysis, we count for something only because of the essential we embody, and if we do not embody that, life is wasted."

—C.G. Jung

AFFIRMATION

I am committed to living a life that I truly love. I will discover and embrace my uniquely beautiful gifts and share them within my world. The purpose of my life is to create that which I am in Essence, into my own beautiful physical Form. I am open and receptive to my Guide within, trusting that living that which I am Called to do is exactly how I want to live my life.

When we begin doing things we enjoy in our lives on a regular basis, this prepares us for the eventuality of welcoming in our innate and essential artistic vision and expressing it in our physical world. When we learn to clear out the clutter and embrace the quiet and solitude we desperately need, then we can create a safe place within ourselves and begin to respect our own essential needs. It is important to live within a healthy and stable environment of our own making, so that we may confidently welcome the joy of opening to our dreams and visions that hold a very special light just for us. It is when all these ingredients come into alignment that we will experience the poignant and powerful moment when we fully commit to ourselves, to allow our own unique, creative expression to emerge and become manifest within our physical world.

This is a turning point, a place of no going back to the old ways we have lived with for so many years. This is the moment where we truly walk into ourselves and become the artists behind our own life's design. This is the time when we finally grasp that it is our right to examine and configure our world from our own positive perspective, no longer allowing the perceptions of our social framework to define and direct us in how we relate and what we do. It is with eyes wide open that we can see fresh relationships amongst things we had never known to be connected. With warmed hearts and inspired minds, we are now learning to express ourselves with a greater sense of clarity and vision. We are very much like the butterfly whose time has come to emerge from within its own cocoon, ready to fly freely out into the world and become the beautiful being we Leaped in here to be. A transformation has taken place, offering us the capacity to attune to our inner directive and respond to the voice of our Guide, Calling us toward our true life's purpose.

This is the moment where we truly walk into ourselves and become the artists behind our own life's design.

No longer can we allow for distractions that cause us to sidestep the light emanating from within us, pulling us off our self-inspired path. Now we must become focused, disregarding the old messages that insisted that we run faster and multitask our way through our days. Now we know, without a doubt, that we have beautiful and important things to do of our own making, and now it is our time to do them. We are not talking about setting even more goals to accomplish, but rather, we are focusing on engaging in those things that create rich meaning and value for ourselves and in turn, reflect our most radiant and essential nature.

Yes, it is true that we human beings are meant to be in motion, but we must be in motion with a defining purpose behind our actions. Scheduling a constant flow of activities just to fill our day is not a goal we need to establish for ourselves. What does matter in goal-setting is that we carefully select how we are going to use our time, so that we may enrich our experience of living. When we embrace the premise that we were born with a mission to fulfill and that we have a Guide within to help us, quite remarkably a pathway will appear, if we open our minds and hearts to *see* it.

Signposts Along the Path

We can look to nature to see this idea at work. There is a balance within our world that allows for the expression of beauty in all things. Without the sun, there would be no life. For our world to exist, plants need to turn that radiant light into chemical energy so that they can grow. As a leaf captures the sun's energy, it turns it into sugar, allowing animals and plants and the entire species of man to exist. Imagine our world without bees, whose job it is to cross-pollinate plants. Without their presence, again, the very existence of humankind would be sorely challenged. And so it goes for hummingbirds and sharks, for trees, weather systems, and humans alike. We are all created with our own unique purpose to fulfill, and if we fail to do this, we will be profoundly upsetting the balance of life on our planet.

As we discussed earlier, do we awaken to our day and announce that today, we are going to fulfill our life's purpose? Or might it be more effective to get up and write a symphony, if that is what we are Called to do? You see, when we live our own specific Calling, we have the capacity to become happy people by expressing the beauty of Essence into a Form, specific to our own creative expression. When we do this, we are experiencing a depth of fulfillment that is purposeful and valuable. When we share our joy and the beauty of what we have created out into our world, we truly are fulfilling not only our own specific reason for living, but supporting the overall purpose of life on Earth.

....

When we share our joy and the beauty of what we have created out into our world, we truly are fulfilling not only our own specific reason for living, but supporting the overall purpose of life on Earth.

....

Perhaps it might help if we think of it in this way. When we drop a pebble into a pond, the ripples of energy radiate outward until they reach the perimeter of land. With the initial action of dropping a pebble into the water, energy is set into motion, creating a secondary effect of the ripples of water touching the shoreline. As it is with the pebble in the pond, so it is with us in our lives. When we focus our intention on creating a song or whatever our special talents allow us to do, there is a secondary response that radiates out into our world, fulfilling the greater purpose for creating a balance of living within all of life. There is nothing that exists on this planet that is not sweetly and profoundly connected to all of life itself. When we write a song and play it for others, they too will be able to enjoy the pleasure and beauty of our expression, thus Octaving the experience beyond the initial action. When our experience of purpose and meaning is accomplished through a joyous act, we deepen the experience, which allows us to continue expanding within our own abilities, and subsequently we are able to share its essence with our world.

Putting It All into Motion

"Nothing happens until something moves."
Albert Einstein

What matters most here is that we begin to put our plans into motion by tapping into what we truly love to do and share it with others. When we do this, we will be impacting every other creature that exists on this Earth in a very positive and beautiful way, by sending out our ripples of energy as we drop our pebble of creativity into the big pond of life. When we set goals for ourselves that fulfill our deep yearning for creative expression, there will always be a more universal benefit to the world as a whole, while assisting us in fulfilling our own purpose for living. As we set our creative Genius into action, a wonderful and unexpected thread of serendipitous events will unfold, with the fore-promised assistance from our Guide. There is a deep respect that must be embraced when creating an expression of the beauty of our Essence into a physical form. It is from within the boldness of taking action, companioned with our alignment with what we are Called to do, that we ignite a dynamic momentum in fulfilling our purpose for living.

PRACTICE—Identifying Your Calling

What is the difference between doing something that you really enjoy and living your Calling? Perhaps we can begin by asking ourselves the following questions and then write down our answers in our journals. Afterward, we will review our responses and see what they tell us.

- If I could never do _____ again, I would feel _____.
  activity   *feeling*

- When I do _____, I feel _____ about myself.
  activity   *feeling*

- When I don't do _____ because I am feeling lazy, this
  makes me feel _____ about myself.
  activity
  feeling

- When someone I care about tells me that my
  doing _____ is foolish and a waste of time, this makes
  me feel _____.
  activity
  feeling

- If someone important to me tells me that I am being selfish by taking time to do _____, I respond to them as
  follows: _____.
  activity

- I get so excited thinking about doing _____!
  activity

- When I know I am doing things that are a part of living
  my true life's purpose, I feel _____.
  feeling

Our Results

Last summer, I was speaking with my very good friend, Julie, and she asked me how I would feel if I didn't actively do my writing. My response was swift, clear, and distinct. I told her that if I couldn't create the time and solitude that I needed to write, I would die. I posed this exact question to a flight attendant named Lisa, as I was traveling from Los Angeles to New York, and she responded with identical words to mine: "I would die."

You see, when we have this degree of intensity and passion for something we want to do, it is a strong indicator that we are tapping into our Calling. In my case, it was true, and even now, as difficult as it is for me some days to actually make myself sit down and write, it would be far more painful if I yielded to my own resistance and didn't push myself through those blocks and just do it.

What is it for you? What Calls out to you so strongly that if you didn't do it, you would feel like the Essence that is in the center of you might just cease to exist, or die? Take some time and look at your answers to the questions above. Be honest with yourself, knowing your answers are your own and that only you need view them. How did they make you feel? As you assess your responses, in time, your personal answers will lead you closer to what you are truly Called to do.

But if at the moment you don't seem to feel strongly about anything, I promise that you will if you continue to use the practices contained in this work. By creating solitude and quiet, taking fifteen minutes a day to do something you enjoy, and learning how to create time that you didn't think you had, you will be on your way to finding that *something* that really sets your heart on fire. You are in the process of preparing, and when that *something* appears, you will recognize it with every fiber of your being and be ready to answer its Call.

PART THREE

Into the Future

Ours is a world of unlimited, creative potential, each one of us infused with an inner directive to engender our lives in our own unique way. By fanning the embers of inspiration that are alight within each one of us, we will kindle our capacity to collectively create a resonantly sustainable world in which we all may live. Acknowledge and respect the hidden grace within your own being; then be bold enough to shine that brilliance out into your world.

20.

Crossroads

We are living in a fascinating time of great and powerful change unfolding within every facet of life all around our planet. Within our remarkable scientific and technological discoveries, some of these changes have the capacity to bring either great opportunity or imminent destruction to our world, contingent upon perception and intent and how it is applied. It is one of life's greatest paradoxes that something so small and innately powerful as an atom can be used for such brilliant benefit or just as readily be transformed into something terrifyingly potent, with the power to annihilate life as we know it. All it takes is one vitally vibrant thought or one nightmarish dream to start those wheels into motion.

As we are catapulted into this twenty-first century, we are being bombarded by the complexities of a fast-paced world and a fierce competition that surrounds us in all that we do. Our economies are deeply compromised and our planet's health is in serious jeopardy, due to our lack of conscience and care. Far too often, we are challenged by our religions and political structures that seem to divide us rather than bringing us together as a united and creative people. Are we, the human collective, so busy trying to simply make it through each day that we have forgotten what it feels like to experience a true sense of joy or a brilliant moment of inspiration? Are we, the people, who have become focused on accumulating rather than creating something uniquely remarkable, fated to become a world dulled by mediocrity?

....

Are we, the human collective, so busy trying to simply make it through each day that we have forgotten what it feels like to experience a true sense of joy or a brilliant moment of inspiration?

....

Unfortunately, it seems that we have forgotten that we are powerfully talented beings born with an enormous transformative potential to create whatever we might dare to imagine within our areas of specialty. We were not destined to Leap into these lives simply to do the bidding of others. We came here to express our own unique Essence, with the assistance of a higher conscience and consciousness, which we now know as our Guide.

However, as we walk the pathway of our lives, distractions abound in many guises, causing good intentions and great ideas to become derailed, inadvertently allowing destructive designs to force themselves upon us. When we lose sight of what we were born to do, we open the doorway for mediocrity to elbow its way in, leaving us weakened and careless. We become quick to self-gratify yet slow to reflect. We prioritize improving our social standing and income flow, and consider our children's accomplishments to be a direct reflection upon our own productive parenting. Have we forgotten that these are our children: soulful individuals born to create their own unique lives, according to their own inner directive? Is it possible that we have truly forgotten that each one of us was born with our own inner initiative to become the highest and best version of ourselves that we could possibly be?

Just how significant is this bankruptcy of self that has insidiously woven its way into the cultures of our world? How far have we allowed ourselves to unravel, to fall apart, losing our innate sense of self and our power to create? For those of us keen enough to observe, we recognize that our Earth is rich with symbolism and metaphor, acting as a mirror, reflecting the greatness as well as the ills of our human condition. By engaging our Genius or by ignoring its resonant Call, humankind has defined the complexion of the world in which we now live, in all its glory and in all its ugliness.

We are poised at a crossroads, with the power to choose how we wish to move forward in our lives and within our world. It is we who bear the responsibility to collectively determine the present and future health and welfare of our families, of our nations, and of our entire planet in all matters of mind, body, and spirit. Yes, we are fully capable of creating a beautiful and sustainable world to love and live in, but we need to awaken our awareness and rekindle our desire to actively choose to do this, both individually and together as one people, for the benefit of all.

21.

Tip and Turn

So, where do we begin? How do we activate and implement our desire to come together as a family of humankind and create a world that reflects our truest Essence expressed into Form? For many people, it seems easier to see what is wrong with our world rather than what is going well, and therein lies one of humanity's greatest challenges and needs: to learn to navigate the circumstances of our lives with a positive and inspired perspective. When we gaze out across the expanse of our planet, what we see and how we respond to it is a reflection of who we are and how we feel about ourselves. When we feel the stirrings of another new day, do we sense a world full of possibility and promise, laced with beauty and grace stretching out before us, or are we already exhausted by our self-directed itinerary and soured by the injustices we will have to suffer? We are all familiar with the glass-half-full or the glass-half-empty metaphor and likely know which part of the glass we drink from.

Think of the girl who suffered one serious illness after another, yet awakened each day excited and enthused to color with her crayons and play with her dolls: she, who later became an influential and inspired fashion designer. What of the boy who had both his legs amputated below the knee when he was a baby, yet went on to compete as a runner in the Olympic Games? Envision the children who were born into abject poverty, yet grew up to become Presidents of the United States. Just imagine the hurdles they had to leap over to become the top leaders of a free and democratic society.

....

When we gaze out across the expanse of our planet, what we see and how we respond to it is a reflection of who we are and how we feel about ourselves.

....

While having a clear determination was important, it took more than their simply pushing forward for them to create compelling meaning and value within their lives. By combining their focus and determination, these children embraced a positive perspective and sense of gratitude along the way, instinctively knowing that there was something vitally important that they were born to do. Despite the diversity of their challenges and their handicaps and suffering, these children did not allow their circumstances to define their lives: Instead, they chose to become one with the promise and possibility that was persistently present, even when the going got tough.

How we choose to live our lives is a matter of essential importance and elementally a matter of perspective. This is the moment where we must choose to Tip and Turn: to decide that when we tip our glass to drink, we know that our glass is half-full and we can turn our perspective toward living in an inspired way. All people experience difficulties and problems in one way or another, but how we respond to our challenges is what defines us. It is in the knowing that there is something we are meant to do, companioned with the power of positivity, that we create the ability to face our personal trials each day, feeling inspired to work hard as we carefully craft the opportunities we choose to embrace.

Yes, some of us may experience nightmarish living circumstances, violence, or ill health, but even under the most extreme circumstances, we have the ability to exercise our gift of free will. In his book, *Man's Search for Meaning,* Viktor Frankl wrote of being incarcerated in a concentration camp, stripped of all human dignities, yet holding onto his power to choose. He wrote " . . . the last of the human freedoms—to choose one's attitude in any given set of circumstances, to choose one's own way." Clearly, the power of choice permeates deeply in the shaping of our lives. In Frankl's words, "Man's inner strength may raise him above his outward fate."

All people experience difficulties and problems in one way or another, but how we respond to our challenges is what defines us.

All people suffer in their own personal ways, but it is in the act of deciding to rise above the dictation of social enculturation and trust our own internal directives that we will begin to experience our world in fresh and positive ways. So, how do we gather up our responses beyond the perimeters of our own personal experience and positively focus them on shaping a beautiful cooperative for all of humanity?

22.

Back to Center

The way in which we respond to the events of our lives is criti-
cally important, not only for ourselves, but also for our families,
our communities, and our world. Whether we view our lives
from a positive perspective of promise and connectivity or walk
our path as a victim, bucking and brawling against the injustices
and inequalities that seem to hold us down, this is an essential
distinction that we must become aware of if we are going to
contribute to creating a world we desire to live in.

It really is very simple. Until we personally engage in living
a life that we have crafted for ourselves, we will experience an
undercurrent of insidious dissatisfaction as our internal light
begins to dim. When we are not aligned with what we truly love
to do, and fail to enjoy a sense of meaning and value, we drag
along a deep and debilitating frustration that gnaws at us from
within our self-abandoned hearts. And when this dissatisfaction
continues to fester, it will predictably morph into an ugly brew
of frustration, jealousy, anger, and potential violence. We will be
unproductively competing for a sense of control in the ebb and
flow of our outer world until we finally come to understand that
that this control we are desperately seeking is merely a phantom
construct, born of a disillusioned and misguided life.

It is a truth that when we are not creatively fulfilled, we are
not at peace within ourselves, and when we are not dynamically

peaceful within our own beings, this is the fractured energy we carry out into our collective world. If this natural, deep yearning to positively create is left unfulfilled within humankind as a whole, this dissatisfaction will serve to direct our collective human behavior down a dark and slippery path, much as we are now witnessing within our straining world. We simply must find our way back to center.

Until we personally engage in living a life that we have crafted for ourselves, we will experience an undercurrent of insidious dissatisfaction as our internal light begins to dim.

In actuality, there is but one primary choice that we will ultimately have to make, both individually and as a collective whole, if we are to live a fulfilling and purposeful life within a healthy and harmonious world. We must choose to do what we love and were born to do, and when we are successfully doing that, we will experience the myriad components of our lives beginning to shift into place. We will become fulfilled and complete at a very personal level, much like a gloriously complex puzzle whose final piece is gracefully slipped into place.

23.

One Voice, One Heart

Creating World Peace challenges nations, religions, busi-nesses, and every individual living on this planet. When we look at another human being and fail to see a beloved sister or brother, there will always be a "them" and an "us."

So, what can we as individuals do to create a world where love and peace prevail? What power do we have to effect a change where the nations of our world actively and respectfully priori-tize the care for all of humanity and for all life forms on this beautiful Earth?

....

To create peace within our world, we need to look within ourselves to that place where conscience and creativity reside.

....

To create peace within our world, we need to look within ourselves to that place where conscience and creativity reside. From within this creative reservoir, the gift of personal expres-sion is born with an exuberance and desire to channel in the joy and love of Dynamic Peace. When we are actively joyful and creatively productive, we are dynamically practicing peace. We become unified within ourselves. When we cooperate with others, rather than compete, we are actively appreciating the differences that make us unique as we choose to join together in a harmonious way. Much like the Butterfly Effect, where the flapping of the butterfly's delicate wings is said to have the power to affect the weather currents on the other side of our planet, so too may our individual joys and beautiful self-expression send wavelengths of creative, loving energy fluttering out into the world.

It is imperative that we collaborate together, recognizing that when we look into the eyes of another, we see that we are alike in the most essential ways. We all require the same ingredients for living—love, health, and inspiration—reminding us that we are truly a bonded community of We rather than a separate and divided You and Me. When we fail to embrace this ideation, the world quickly becomes an aggressive place where selfishness, fear, competition, violence, and brutality lead the way.

To create a world that reflects a brotherhood and sisterhood of humankind, a world that holds a deep respect for all life on our glorious planet, we must choose to acknowledge the grace and Essence of every other human being as being valuable and precious. We must recognize that their Essence is our Essence. There is only One Essence, and from this Wave of non-physical existence, we are all born. As we Particulate into our individuated selves and Leap into our lives, we all share the same purpose for living. We must remember and honor this. When we respect others, we respect ourselves, and when we nurture ourselves by doing what we love, we are embracing our true purpose for living: We are creating that which we are in Essence into a beautiful and precious human life.

....

There is only One Essence, and from this Wave of non-physical existence, we are all born.

....

24.

Closing Thoughts

When I was a very little girl, I remember the scorching outrage that burned within my little body when I overheard an adult discussion concerning corporal punishment and the death penalty. My tender mind could not comprehend why anyone would think that they had the right to take away another person's life, despite whatever grievous transgression had been committed. I thought it would be far more productive to first look within, before spewing blame and judgment out onto another. I also believed that if they were not so unhappy inside of themselves, they would never be able to commit such a grievous act. I felt a deep sadness for the person who had been wronged and also felt badly for the one who launched the attack. For better or worse, this was my own unique perspective, fresh out of my young heart and mind, not a philosophical ideology I had heard previously expressed. It simply was a component in the nature of my being, my own intrinsic ethos.

It seems we are launched into our lives as highly developed and soulful little creatures, wrapped in these miraculous bodies of babes. We come fully loaded with an imprint of indigenous talent and inclination, with an open and loving heart. We are fresh and bright. We are love. We are peace. *We Are.* Cocooned in the protection of our enlightened infancy, we are safeguarded for a nanosecond from the intensely complex lives that fan out ahead of us, still untainted by the division and conflict that seem to define the architectural mindscape of our current world.

Though we may have forgotten how miraculously open and embracing we were when we leaped across that gauzy threshold into our lives, we still do have the unlimited capacity to open our hearts, expand our minds, and tear down our internal and external walls that serve to divide us, damage us, and foolishly define us. We are powerful beings, born with an enormous, transformative potential to create whatever we might imagine within our lives. We were not born to be defined by our political perspectives, nor controlled by our religious beliefs we choose to honor. We are not our jobs; we are not the money we earn. We are not to be branded by the condition of our mental, emotional, or physical health, nor are we to be defined by our marital status, sexual orientation, race, gender, intelligence quotient, or body size.

We are fresh and bright. We are love. We are peace. We Are.

We are women and we are men. Together, we have sons and daughters whom we love and cherish. We are creative and compassionate; we are kind and generous when we are bold enough to no longer feel the need to posture and pretend. Yes, we are a confluence of paradoxes, yet ultimately, we all have one essential element that we share in common. We are all the physical, human expression of that which we are in Essence and we share the commonality of being humanly creative beings given this breathtaking gift of life.

As we launch ourselves into our auspicious and most optimistic future, may we unite as a family of humankind, respecting and embracing our unique differences, understanding that we are all resonantly luminous particles in this Quantum Wave of wondrous humanity. Together, may we each expand into the brilliance of who we were born to be, and collectively, may we flourish within the grace of Dynamic Peace for all.

About the Author

photo by Zephyr Eve Beck

Heather McCloskey Beck is an inspirational author and speaker, musician, and founder of the global peace movement *Peace Flash*. Dedicated to creating Dynamic Peace within our world, Heather is a columnist for *The Huffington Post* and frequently speaks to audiences across the United States. With a growing following on her Facebook pages that has surpassed one million fans, Beck offers both virtual and on-site workshops and events to inspire people to create lives they truly love.

To find out more, please visit her online at www.Heather McCloskeyBeck.com and on her Facebook Author Page facebook.com/HeatherMcCloskeyBeckAuthor

To Our Readers

Conari Press, an imprint of Red Wheel/Weiser, publishes books on topics ranging from spirituality, personal growth, and relationships to women's issues, parenting, and social issues. Our mission is to publish quality books that will make a difference in people's lives—how we feel about ourselves and how we relate to one another. We value integrity, compassion, and receptivity, both in the books we publish and in the way we do business.

Our readers are our most important resource, and we appreciate your input, suggestions, and ideas about what you would like to see published.

Visit our website at *www.redwheelweiser.com* to learn about our upcoming books and free downloads, and be sure to go to *www.redwheelweiser.com/newsletter/* to sign up for newsletters and exclusive offers.

You can also contact us at *info@rwwbooks.com.*

Conari Press
an imprint of Red Wheel/Weiser, LLC
665 Third Street, Suite 400
San Francisco, CA 94107